The Pow

To Alison
for the privilege and joy of sharing her life

The power of the
force
The spirituality of the *Star Wars*® films

David Wilkinson

A LION BOOK

Published by
Lion Publishing plc
Sandy Lane West, Oxford, England
www.lion-publishing.co.uk
ISBN 0 7459 4402 7

First edition 2000
10 9 8 7 6 5 4 3 2 1 0

Acknowledgments
pp. 29–30: time line taken from Bill Slavicsek, *A Guide to the
Star Wars Universe*, Boxtree, 1995

The following words/phrases are proprietary
names or are registered in the United Kingdom
or as Community trade marks:
Anakin Skywalker
Artoo-Detoo (R2-D2)
Chewbacca
Ewok
Luke Skywalker
May the Force be with you
Obi-Wan Kenobi
Princess Leia Organa
See-Threepio (C-3PO)
Star Wars
Yoda, the Jedi Master

A catalogue record for this book is available
from the British Library

Typeset in 11.5/16 Berkeley Oldstyle
Printed and bound in Finland

Contents

Preface

The university professor looked at me, horrified, as though I had committed an unforgivable sin. 'Why?' he asked, in the style of parents objecting to some naughty child's action. I had just told him I was writing a book on the spirituality of *Star Wars*. Perhaps he was unable to see how *Star Wars* and spirituality were at all connected. Perhaps he felt *Star Wars* was just too popular – worthy of merchandising, but not serious academic study. However, more than likely, he had never even heard of *Star Wars*!

I gave four reasons as justification. First, my own enjoyment of the *Star Wars* movies and the way they seemed to resonate with my Christian faith. As I began to research the background of the movies, especially the motivation and ideas of George Lucas, I discovered the reasons why there was such a resonance.

Second, from my background in science and theology I was interested in how these subjects were treated in popular culture. *Star Wars* uses both, and their relationship, within its own story. Here was a discussion of science and theology that was not confined to the lecture theatre or church, but touched everything from the back of a cereal box to multimillion-dollar businesses.

Third, I was working at a church with a large number of people in their teens, twenties and thirties who were as fascinated as I was with *Star Wars*. Some were Christians, some were of other faiths, some were of no faith at all, but *Star Wars* raised religious questions for us all. In addition, for the last six months I had been speaking about this material in different contexts – from schools and universities to television and radio. During this time I had been impressed by both the popularity of *Star Wars* with highly diverse groups of people, and by the seriousness with which they wanted to discuss spiritual questions.

The fourth reason was by far the most important. It gives my children some street cred to know that their father is writing on *Star Wars*! As always they have been a constant source of joy and distraction in the writing of this book. My wife Alison has read the manuscript and brought her own considerable theological ability to the questions. Without her, none of this would have been possible. James Cook also read the manuscript and checked the references.

Early in this project, I gathered together a group of people of various ages to discuss the movies and explore the questions that they raise. I am thankful to Liz Powell, Ian Kent, Ajay and Karen George, Margaret Taylor, Lucy Brooke, Jamie Probin, Alison Hulse and Alison Wilkinson for their ideas and shared enjoyment of the movies.

Finally, to Elm Hall Drive Methodist Church, thank you for your support and encouragement, which makes all my writing possible.

David Wilkinson
Liverpool
15 July 1999

1
Every journey
has a first step

I did not see *Star Wars* when it first appeared in 1977. I have never owned a lightsabre, never played with a Ewok toy village, and never fancied Princess Leia. Some of my friends did and still do. I am not a *Star Wars* fanatic, but I share with others of my generation an excitement with the movies, videos and games. Part of it is nostalgia for my teenage years, but part of it goes much deeper. This book is an attempt to explore the attraction of *Star Wars* and to have fun while doing it.

I know that there is a widely held view that every thirteen-year-old marvelled at the opening scene of *Star Wars* – the small spaceship being pursued by the vast Star Destroyer – and their life was changed for ever. This thirteen-year-old, however, was more interested in football than cinema. In fact, apart from an occasional visit to see films such as *Chitty Chitty Bang Bang* and *The Land That Time Forgot*, going to the cinema was an unusual experience. Looking back, those films were probably representative of what cinema was like at the time!

However, I did like reading books and I saw in the bookshop a paperback edition of *Star Wars: From the Adventures of Luke Skywalker* (as it was then titled). I thought I would read about this movie that all my friends were talking about. The experience was not life-changing but fun. I loved the story. It was not a classic in literary terms, but the story grabbed me: a young hero, a courageous princess, good and evil, spaceships and swords, and – best of all – the good guys won. It was fantasy, but at the same time contained very powerful ideas and themes.

Perhaps that was what I found so fascinating. At this stage I had not been excited by the special effects; that would come later. The story and the ideas it dealt with came first. Within my own teenage experience those ideas began to resonate: there was more to life than just what we see; there is hope, and evil is real. I was not especially religious, but I was beginning to ask questions. Did God exist or did science disprove him? Would the world be destroyed in a nuclear war? Did the evil portrayed in occult or horror stories really exist? They were simple questions, and part of growing up in the seventies.

Star Wars seemed to touch on these questions. It was good entertainment but it was more than that. It never gave answers but it gave permission to ask the questions. As I moved from teenager to astrophysicist to theologian the questions changed their form, but they were still there. As I wrote on the early universe and on the existence of extraterrestrial life, the questions were there also. Some suggested that Stephen Hawking's theory of quantum gravity, which explained how the universe came into being, seemed to rule out any belief in a creator God: was this true? In the area of extraterrestrial intelligence I saw that both in the scientific quest and in science fiction, people were looking at questions of purpose, identity, fear and salvation.

Star Wars remained a fun way of exploring those types of questions. I do not mean that, after watching one of the movies on video, I would immediately hold a philosophy seminar with my five-year-old son. But it did reinforce the importance of those questions.

It is a long way from the desert planet of Tatooine to the city of Liverpool. Yet, as I worked with a church in the city, I encountered similar questions. Where did hope come from when – in the lives of many – poverty, illness and death had to be faced? How could I deal with the evil in other people and in myself? Could I do anything about such evil? *Star Wars* and other movies allowed me to take those questions out of the seriousness of the reality of the situation and think about them in the freedom of the fantasy of fiction.

I certainly did not start spouting '*Star Wars* wisdom'. On the wall of my office is a poster entitled, 'All I need to know about life I learned from *Star Wars*'. It collects such gems of wisdom as 'The possibility of successfully navigating an asteroid field is approximately 3,720 to 1,' and 'Always let the Wookiee win!' Not the most helpful words of wisdom for inner-city Liverpool. Neither would you say to a student contemplating suicide, 'Try not. Do. Or do not. There is no try,' or to a number of young men late on a Friday night outside a pub, 'Anger, fear and aggression lead to the dark side.'

Nevertheless, *Star Wars* allowed a relaxed contemplation of questions about God, evil and hope. That was true not only for me, but also for the teenagers, students and young adults with whom I worked. Some of these people had only seen *Star*

Wars on television or video, years after its initial release.

It has never transformed my life, but it does fascinate me. I am not interested in endless *Star Wars* trivia, but I have had many conversations with a diverse range of people, from children to academics, who are also fascinated by it.

Sir Alec Guinness, objecting to the way that people have taken *Star Wars* too seriously, commented, 'when the film was first shown, it had a freshness, also a sense of moral good fun'.[1] Those who want to analyse it must never forget that, whether in movie, book or game form, it is meant to provide excitement and fun. Some who have criticised it have made the mistake of ignoring that. Yet for something to be exciting it needs to touch the spirit. That sense of the moral or the religious is, I believe, key to its success.

The success of *Star Wars*

Star Wars is simply the most successful series of films, videos, books and action toys ever. The original three films have grossed $1.8 billion and the merchandising $4.5 billion.

In terms of its popularity, *Star Wars: A New Hope* is one of the biggest movies of all time. Recently the Hollywood trade magazine, *Variety*, produced a table showing how much money films have made at American box offices after adjusting for inflation.[2] The top three were:

1. *Gone with the Wind* (1939) $1.3 billion
2. *Snow White and the Seven Dwarfs* (1937) $1 billion
3. *Star Wars* (1977) $825 million

Even James Cameron's smash hit of recent years *Titanic* (1998) at $600 million does not come close.

In May 1999, the prequel to the trilogy of *Star Wars*, *The Empire Strikes Back* and *Return of the Jedi* appeared on US cinema screens. *The Phantom Menace* was dubbed the most eagerly awaited movie of the twentieth century. Accompanied by huge merchandising of toys, computer games and books, it was launched with vast interest from the media worldwide. Such is the scale of *The Phantom Menace* that, in order to break even at the box office, it had to become one of the top ten grossing movies of all time! It will be followed by Episodes II and III of the prequel series over the next few years.

Star Wars has a truly worldwide appeal. When Roger Enrico, the boss of Pepsi, signed a $2 billion deal in 1996 to market products tied in to *The Phantom Menace* he said, 'This will allow us to connect with virtually every consumer in the world.'[3] He may have been overstating his case, but not too much.

Shakespeare in space or sad psychosis?

One of the fascinating things about liking *Star Wars* is that it does not have the 'geekdom' of liking other forms of science fiction. To confess to liking *Star Trek* runs the risk of being viewed as someone who dresses up as Mr Worf on a regular basis. *Star Trek* has its own committed audience and fans tend to learn Klingon and go to numerous conventions. *Star Wars* is far more wide-ranging in its appeal. Of course, some fans do dress up in silly costumes, but there are many fans of *Star*

Wars who do not like science fiction and cannot stand *Star Trek* or *Dr Who*.

Those who saw it first in childhood are now in their twenties and thirties. A recent magazine claimed that there now exists a generation of young adults with well-paid jobs and children who can name every character in the trilogy. Sometimes they speak about it in religious terms.

Matt Bielby, editor of *Total Film*, wrote, 'For anyone whose formative years took place in the late seventies, *Star Wars* is a religious experience.'[4] *Clerks'* director Kevin Smith called *Star Wars* 'the biggest thing that ever did or ever will happen to our generation',[5] and Ian Nathan, editor of *Empire* magazine, said, 'it defined modern perception of cinema… It changed my life for the better. And I knew millions of others were feeling exactly the same thing at exactly the same moment. *Star Wars* became part of us.'[6]

Some obviously go to extremes. Bret Calltharp, an accountant from Florida, after watching a trailer for *The Phantom Menace* which he had downloaded from the internet, said, 'Afterwards I sat at my screen and just wept. My wife was holding me, trying to understand. It was the culmination of twenty-three years of my life… it was as if someone deeply religious who has only ever known of the New Testament finally gets to read the Old Testament.'[7] The phrase 'get a life' is easy to use at this point!

Sir Alec Guinness tells of being approached by a child who had seen *Star Wars* over a hundred times and his proud mother. Sir Alec asked him not to watch it any more, which provoked an unfavourable reaction from both the child and the mother. In his own defence Sir Alec writes that he hopes that the child 'is not living in a fantasy world of second-hand, childish banalities'.[8]

Others have criticised the extreme reactions *Star Wars* produces. The journalist Sarah Vine commented, 'Truth is, you really do need to be a male aged between thirteen and seventeen, with no girlfriend and a pivotal role in your local Dungeons and Dragons coven, to still get excited about *Star Wars*.'[9] A similar line was taken by Gabrielle Morris who called interest in *Star Wars* a mass nerd psychosis, 'a form of male autism for dysfunctional boys'.[10]

Others have doubted whether *Star Wars*' appeal will endure. Dale Pollock, writing in 1990, said, 'the audience for *Star Wars* movies seems to have grown up… Today's movie audiences have also become more cynical and jaded; Tim Burton's dark vision of *Batman* is light years from the upbeat morality play Lucas devised for *Star Wars*.'[11] The last ten years have proved him wrong. The 'dark vision' of *Batman* took on a new morality under director Joel Schumacher, and the enduring appeal of *Star Wars* in all its forms has grown.

Star Wars has come to 'represent one of the great myths of our time'.[12] The film critic Richard Rayner summed it up when he wrote, 'I left the cinema thrilled. It was obvious that, in essence, *Star Wars* was an old-fashioned Saturday morning space-adventure serial, executed with dazzling special effects, and with powerful story elements drawn from so many other works… the film felt fresh, vigorous and, above all, innocent. And if its simplistic moral message fed a nostalgia for lost values, it signalled a much-needed return to the purity of what cinema was supposed to do: move the audience, and awaken a sense of visual awe.'[13] This it continues to do.

The British actor Brian Blessed goes so far as to liken George Lucas, the creator of *Star Wars*, to Shakespeare. He says, '*Star Wars*, *The Empire Strikes Back* and *Return of the Jedi* are the three finest films I've ever seen. I feel that *Star Wars* does more for the civilised development of the human race than any other piece of art in the world.'[14]

These are grand words for movies that have sometimes been derided. Indeed, they are not perfect. Watching the original movies now makes you aware of the cheesy dialogue, somewhat ropy acting and one or two classic mistakes. For example in *Star Wars*, as the stormtroopers on the Death Star rush into the room where the droids are hiding, one of them bashes his head quite severely on the door frame! Only in the widescreen version will you be able to see a man in a green shirt somewhat miraculously standing behind Han and Chewbacca as they blast away in the *Millennium Falcon*!

Why does *Star Wars* have such an appeal? There are many answers to this and in order to see them we will have to review its history and the motives behind it. The theological elements inherent in it are key to its appeal. It raises questions about spirituality and ultimately is dependent on belief in God.

I will use the term 'spirituality' to refer to spiritual quality or, more specifically, the recognition and response to the spiritual. Dale Pollock, in his biography of George Lucas, writes, 'The message of *Star Wars* is religious: God isn't dead; he's there if you want him to be.'[15]

2

The beginning

George Lucas was twenty-seven years old when he tried to sell a thirteen-page story idea to both Universal and United Artists. Up to this point, the young film director had only achieved commercial success with one film, *American Graffiti*, which told the story of teenage rites of passage.

This new story idea was very different. It began, 'the story of Mace Windu, a revered Jedi-bendu of the Opuchi, who was related to Usby C.J. Thape, padawaan learner of the famed Jedi'; not perhaps the most gripping or understandable of opening lines! It was set in the twenty-third century and its title gradually evolved into *The Star Wars*. Neither Universal nor United Artists wanted to go with such a concept, but eventually Twentieth Century Fox agreed to give Lucas $50,000 to write a screenplay, and $100,000 to direct it.

'Every saga has a beginning...'

The first screenplay took a year to develop and was finished in May 1974. In it Luke Skywalker was an old general and Han

Solo a huge green-skinned monster. They fought against an evil emperor who was subverting power, a character modelled on Richard Nixon. The second screenplay (January 1975) had the title *Adventures of the Starkiller, Episode One of the Star Wars*. This script included a quest for an object called the Kiber Crystal whose energy field was in charge of the destiny of all life. Even at this early stage of development we can see Lucas's fascination with theological motifs and questions of spirituality. The script contained the line, 'In the times of greatest despair there shall come a saviour, and he shall be known as "The Son of Suns".' Although this reference was dropped before the final version, the themes of hope and redemption are there, and other biblical imagery.

In May 1975, Lucas sent the script for what was now called *The Star Wars* to Alan Ladd, Jr, at Twentieth Century Fox. The opening blurb described *The Star Wars* as 'an engaging human drama set in a fantasy world that paralyses the imagination... A story not only for children, but for anyone who likes a grand tale of wonder on an epic scale... filled with marvels and strange terrors, moral warmth and, most of all, pure excitement.'[16] In this version, for the first time, appeared the famous line of 'May the Force be with you,' paralleling the Christian blessing of 'May the Lord be with you.'

His script was over 500 pages in length, almost five times too long for one movie. He divided it up into three parts, and put two parts away for sequels. Instead of being set in the future, Lucas now set his story in a technological society in the past, and in a galaxy 'far, far away'.

Casting began and Lucas worked jointly with Brian de Palma who was casting for *Carrie* (1976). They were both looking for a group of young actors. Of the main actors eventually cast, Harrison Ford had been in *American Graffiti* but was working as a carpenter, and Mark Hamill and Carrie Fisher came from relative obscurity. Sir Alec Guinness received an unsolicited script and, because he became fascinated by the story, agreed to take the part of Obi-Wan Kenobi.

It is difficult to overstate Lucas's commitment to *Star Wars*. By the time that *Star Wars* was fully accepted by Fox in December 1975, Lucas had already invested $1 million of his own money into the project. This was the money he had made from *American Graffiti*.

Lucas believed in it but there were plenty who did not. Alan Ladd, Jr, called it 'possibly the greatest picture ever made' when trying to justify it to the Fox board, but Fox were very unsure of the film's commercial prospects.[17] In fact, when Lucas asked for an increase in his director's fee, Fox instead offered him the sequel and prequel rights, and the subsequent merchandising to the films. As they were not convinced that *Star Wars* would be a success at the box office they were happy to give away these rights, unsure that any further movies would be made. In that decision they lost several billion dollars and allowed Lucas to set up his own empire of film-making.

Gary Kurtz, producer of *Star Wars*, said, 'At the time... we had no idea if there was a market for it or not – it was just speculation.'[18]

Twentieth Century Fox were not the only pessimists around. During production at Elstree studios the British technicians poked fun at this strange space opera, actors such as Harrison Ford complained about the script, Sir Alec Guinness objected to being killed off halfway through, the remote-controlled droid R2-D2 kept walking into walls, and there were a number of technical problems and delays on the special effects. Before the end of filming Mark Hamill had a serious car crash and required plastic surgery, resulting in Lucas having to film some scenes without him.

All this was against the background that science fiction in movies was rather unfashionable. It looked as though, if *Star Wars* survived at all, it would be a very modest success. When Lucas showed the first rough cut of the movie with no music and some of the special effects missing to a group of fellow directors, he was faced with embarrassment, giggles and ridicule. In particular, Brian de Palma said that it was one of the worst things he had ever seen, and during lunch kept making jokes about the 'Almighty Force'. Only Steven Spielberg seemed to be at all encouraging. Even when the trailers were shown in the movie theatres, many people greeted them with laughter and ridicule. Not the most hopeful of beginnings to the biggest series of movies ever.

Star Wars: Episode IV

Yet when *Star Wars* opened in thirty-two cinemas on 25 May 1977 in New York and Los Angeles, people queued for two hours before the first 10 a.m. showing. John Williams' soundtrack and cutting-edge special effects gave power to the story, which had changed radically since Lucas's first treatment.

There will be few readers who do not know the outline of the story but, for the few, here it is. Lucas viewed *Star Wars: A New Hope* as Episode IV in a nine-part space epic. Setting the story 'a long time ago in a galaxy far, far away' he employed an opening title scrolling text reminiscent of the old *Flash Gordon* serials to introduce the audience to the setting.

Princess Leia (played by Carrie Fisher) attempts to smuggle to the Rebel Alliance plans of the evil Empire's ultimate weapon, the Death Star. Captured by the sinister Darth Vader – and somewhat hindered by an embarrassing hairstyle, reminiscent of wearing two bagels over the ears – she sends the plans with the stocky and all-purpose droid, R2-D2, who is accompanied by a protocol droid, C-3PO. R2-D2's mission is to find the last of the Jedi Knights, Obi-Wan Kenobi (played by Sir Alec Guinness). The Jedi Knights were once guardians of the peace and justice in the galaxy, using the mysterious Force as their source of power. Darth Vader was a Jedi Knight who turned to the dark side of the Force and used its dark power to exterminate the Jedi.

The droids eventually fall into the possession of Owen and Beru Lars and their nephew, Luke Skywalker (played by Mark Hamill). They own a farm on the desert planet of Tatooine, but Luke is frustrated that he cannot leave like all his friends and learn to be a pilot. R2-D2 escapes to find Obi-Wan Kenobi and Luke pursues him, fearful of his uncle's anger at the loss. The old Jedi Knight introduces Luke to the power of the Force, pressuring him to join the mission of taking the plans to the Rebel Alliance.

As the stormtroopers of the Empire pursue them, they hire an odd flying saucer called the *Millennium Falcon*, piloted by the lovable rogue Han Solo (played by Harrison Ford) and what appears to be a walking carpet, but is really a Wookiee called Chewbacca.

Captured by the Death Star, they rescue Princess Leia, who then has to save them, and through the self-sacrifice of Obi-Wan Kenobi they escape to the Rebel base. The plans are delivered, analysed and show a weakness in the Death Star: a badly designed exhaust port. A direct hit on this will destroy the huge machine and no doubt lose the Death Star architects their job!

In the battle that ensues between Empire and Rebels, Luke, by trusting the Force, is able to deliver the death blow, and the Rebels are victorious.

The *Variety* review of *Star Wars* on the day it was released summed up its power: 'Like a breath of fresh air *Star Wars* sweeps away the cynicism that has in recent years obscured the concepts of valour, dedication and honour… in *Star Wars* the people remain the masters of the hardware, thereby striking a more resonant note of empathy and hope. This is the kind of film in which the audience, first entertained, can later walk out feeling good all over.'[19]

Audiences were encountering not just a science-fiction movie, but a movie that was about some fundamental ideas. Hope and the tension between technology and the human spirit were at its core. Alongside this, it was exciting good fun. Irvin Kershner, who would later direct the next instalment of the saga, *The Empire Strikes Back*, tells of taking his ten-year-old son to see *Star Wars* and being amazed by his reaction: 'At first his mouth dropped open in amazement, and he looked bewildered. Then he began laughing and was on the edge of his seat the whole time. I wondered why he was so excited. Gradually I got caught up too.'[20]

The movie, which two studios had rejected and a third had severe doubts about, eventually collected ten nominations for

Academy Awards, won five Oscars and had grossed $430 million worldwide by the end of 1979.

Lucas enjoyed the success. He had conceived the idea, written the script, directed it and put his life and money into it. On the opening weekend, however, he took a holiday in Hawaii with Steven Spielberg and their two families. As the two directors built a sandcastle on the beach they talked about an idea which would eventually become *Raiders of the Lost Ark* – but before that could be done there was the small matter of the *Star Wars* sequel, Episode V.

The Empire Strikes Back

The money that Lucas had made through *Star Wars* enabled him to personally finance the next episode, leaving Fox simply to distribute it. Employing writers Leigh Brackett and Lawrence Kasdan, and the director Irvin Kershner, Lucas had less of the pressure than with *Star Wars*. However he remained very much a hands-on executive producer, providing the original story and wanting to safeguard the story development.

Filming started in March 1979 in the frozen expanses of Norway. A severe winter hampered much of the film-making, while back in England and in the US the budget spiralled to $33 million. The movie contained an enormous 600 special-effects shots, twice as many as in *Star Wars*.

The Empire Strikes Back follows on from the plot of *Star Wars*. A new Rebel base on the ice planet of Hoth is located and destroyed by the Empire. The Rebels escape and go their separate ways. Luke, directed by a vision of Obi-Wan Kenobi, goes to the swamp planet of Dagobah. There he meets Yoda, a small, 800-year-old Jedi Master with an inverted style of speech. He is a muppet character with eyes modelled on the eyes of Albert Einstein! Yoda attempts to instruct Luke in the ways of the Force.

The director, Irvin Kershner, was a vegetarian and a student of Zen Buddhism and was fascinated by the philosophical implications of the Force. As a result, Yoda reflects many of the precepts of Buddhism in his instruction about the Force.

Meanwhile, Leia, Han, Chewbacca and the droids head for Cloud City and walk straight into a trap set by Darth Vader and a bounty hunter called Boba Fett, who quickly achieved cult status with many fans. Lando Calrissian (played by Billy Dee Williams), Cloud City governor and old friend of Han, is forced to cooperate in the plot. Introducing a black character to *Star Wars* was, in part, a response to charges of racism.

In *Star Wars* there were no black characters, but Darth Vader's voice was supplied by the black actor, James Earl Jones. Moreover, Darth Vader's evil was symbolised by his black costume. In fairness to Lucas, it is important to point out that the barring of the two droids from the space cantina in *Star Wars* makes an explicit comment on racism.

Luke goes to help his friends and faces Vader. In the duel he loses his hand and gains a father, Vader revealing that, before his corruption by the dark side, he had fathered Luke. Rather than giving in to the dark side, Luke chooses death by throwing himself off the gantry. His fall is cushioned and he survives. Han Solo is not as fortunate, being frozen in carbon and sent as a wall decoration to the gangster, Jabba the Hutt. Leia and Lando escape and rescue Luke. The ending sets up the third episode. The power of the narrative is such that, at the end of a 1980 preview of *The Empire Strikes Back* in New York, a man stood up in the packed auditorium and shouted, 'Start Part Three!' The man was Isaac Asimov, the noted science-fiction author.

When *The Empire Strikes Back* was released on 21 May 1980, people queued for three days before the opening. It sold more than $300 million worth of tickets in its initial release. The *Variety* review of 14 May 1980 called it a place 'where good and evil are never confused and the righteous will always win'.[21] It also commented on Lucas's use of other movie elements including aerial dogfights, Wild West shoot-outs, sword fights and war-movie parallels such as the attack on infantry in trenches.

The Empire Strikes Back received fourteen Academy Award nominations and carried off six Oscars; in some territories it earned more than *Star Wars*.

However, before Lucas could begin Episode VI he turned his attention back to the conversation over a sandcastle in Hawaii. With Steven Spielberg directing, he produced and co-wrote the story for *Raiders of the Lost Ark*, which was released in 1981.

The story bore some of the characteristic Lucas touches, already developed in *Star Wars*. It concerned an unscrupulous academic playboy in a quest for the legendary ark of the covenant. There were clearly defined good guys and bad guys and supernatural powers. Harrison Ford, in the title role as Indiana Jones, played the hero on a quest. For all his failings, Indiana Jones had a developed sense of right and wrong. Spielberg wanted him to be an alcoholic but Lucas felt that this would undermine his hero role.

The triumph of good and the power of forces beyond us returned yet again in Episode VI of the unfolding saga of *Star Wars*.

Return of the Jedi

Filmed under the pseudonym of *Blue Harvest*, Lucas originally announced the title as *Revenge of the Jedi*. It was a clever ploy to mislead the manufacturers of illegal merchandise, and after all, he claimed, the true fans should know that revenge does not fit with Jedi philosophy.

In contrast to the two years it took to write Episode IV, Lucas wrote the first draft of *Return of the Jedi* in four weeks. Here we see a much more mature Luke as a Jedi Knight. He rescues Han from the slimy clutches of Jabba, with the help of Leia, Chewbacca, Lando and the droids.

Rejoining the Rebels they learn that the Empire is building a second Death Star, inevitably 'even more powerful than the first'. For those interested, this time it was 160 km across with 30,000 turbolaser cannons! A forcefield generated on the Moon of Endor protects the Death Star. Luke, Leia et al. attempt to neutralise the forcefield with the help of small teddy bears, Ewoks, who live in the lush forests of the moon.

In fact the evil Emperor Palpatine and Darth Vader have set a trap for both Luke and the Rebel fleet. The Emperor and Vader attempt to turn Luke to the dark side of the Force. Defeating Vader in a duel, Luke refuses to kill him and give in to the dark side. In return Vader saves Luke by killing the Emperor at the cost of his own life. The Death Star is destroyed, Leia is revealed to be Luke's sister, thus resolving the love triangle with Han Solo, and all is well in the galaxy.

It is interesting to note that Harrison Ford wanted Han Solo to die at the end of *Return of the Jedi*. Lucas would not agree, arguing that it would ruin the ending of what was intended to be a positive film.

Return of the Jedi premiered on 25 May 1983, six years to the day after the original *Star Wars*. This time there were queues for eight days before the opening and it became the third most successful film of all time behind *Star Wars* and Spielberg's *E.T.* Within a month it had grossed $70 million.

The critics were not as kind this time, criticising Lucas for an over-reliance on special effects and *Variety* memorably called Darth Vader an 'oversized gas pump'.[22]

At this point Lucas took a long break from the *Star Wars* saga, looking at other projects before returning to Episodes I, II and III. With Spielberg, he made the sequels to *Raiders of the Lost Ark*: *Indiana Jones and the Temple of Doom* (1984) and *Indiana Jones and the Last Crusade* (1989). In this last movie the quest for the Holy Grail and its supernatural powers was combined with a father/son relationship played beautifully on screen by Ford and Sean Connery. Again these were key Lucas themes: a hero quest, the supernatural, and dysfunctional families.

The return of *Star Wars*

By the mid-1990s the *Star Wars* trilogy had earned $1.3 billion in movies and videos and more than $3 billion in merchandising. However, Lucas wanted to return to the three original movies before the release of Episode I.

In the seventies and early eighties Lucas did not have all the technology he needed to fully realise his vision. With advances in technology he was able to improve Episodes IV, V and VI, and augment them. New visual effects were added, the soundtrack was remastered and the original negative was restored.

Lucas also wanted them to come out together, rather like old matinée serials, and so the three movies, called special editions, were re-released within weeks of each other in 1997. Dale Pollock's statement that the *Star Wars* audience had grown up and preferred more cynical movies was demolished as the re-released *Star Wars* took $36 million on its opening weekend. It reclaimed the record of the biggest-grossing film of all time which it originally set in 1978. Those who had seen it the first time around were joined by a new generation of *Star Wars* fans, who had never seen it before on the big screen.

This re-release set the scene for the first of the prequels that would appear in 1999. This, as we shall see in a later chapter, deals with the fall of Luke's father Anakin and his transformation into Darth Vader. Episodes II and III are expected to appear in the next few years, although Lucas seems to be indicating that he will not make Episodes VII to IX, which would have told the story after *Return of the Jedi*.

A brief history of *Star Wars* time

It may be helpful at this stage to have an overview of the story that Lucas has constructed. The development of the story has been carefully thought out, and much of it has been in Lucas's mind from the beginning.

Bill Slavicsek in *A Guide to the Star Wars Universe*[23] puts together the movies with games and novels to construct the following time line. It is characterised as years before the time of the events of *Star Wars* (BSW) and years after the events of *Star Wars* (ASW):

25,000+ BSW	Old Republic, first galaxy-wide government is formed; Jedi Knights appear, peace

896 BSW	Yoda, the Jedi Master born
200 BSW	Chewbacca the Wookiee born
60 BSW	Obi-Wan Kenobi born
55 BSW	Anakin Skywalker born
35 BSW	Clone Wars end
29 BSW	Han Solo born

Fall of the Republic – dark period of corruption and social injustice sweeps through the Republic, paving the way for Senator Palpatine's rise to power

18 BSW	Luke and Leia born and placed into hiding

Anakin becomes Darth Vader
Jedi Knights hunted and killed
Palpatine becomes Emperor
Empire formed; first stirring of rebellion

Star Wars	First Death Star destroyed at the Battle of Yavin
3 ASW	Events of *The Empire Strikes Back*, Battle of Hoth takes place
4 ASW	Events of *Return of the Jedi*, Galactic civil war ends with the Battle of Endor, New Republic formed; Imperial remnants fight on

This is the outline of the story which has transformed modern cinema.

3

'Don't underestimate the Force'

Recently I found myself in a television studio doing an interview on the significance of *Star Wars*. On my right was someone unfairly introduced as a 'Scottish Jedi Knight'. He was in fact a devoted *Star Wars* fanatic, watching one part of the trilogy every Sunday afternoon. *Star Wars* had had a profound effect on his life and he tried to live his life following the Force. To my left was a media academic who had been invited to act as the cynic, deriding any importance of *Star Wars*. He was entertaining with references to 'Pizza the Hutt' and the fact that he had never seen *Star Wars* all the way through because he kept falling asleep.

I felt myself in the middle, both physically and in terms of the argument. *Star Wars* can become an obsession, but we do need to recognise its success and the effect it has had on modern cinema.

The success of *Star Wars* has had a huge effect, not least of course on George Lucas himself. He owns nearly 6,000 acres of California, and 400 miles north of Hollywood he has created Skywalker Ranch at a cost estimated to be $200 million. It is the heart of Lucas's empire, home to his companies and 1,800 employees, where technical and administrative buildings blend into the carefully crafted hills and lakes. Skywalker Ranch stands as a witness to the legacy of *Star Wars* and the independence of Lucas, who is able to create and finance his films rather than being controlled by the big Hollywood studios.

Yet the effect of *Star Wars* on the world outside Skywalker Ranch, and in particular on the movie industry, has been colossal. Three elements are especially significant.

The audience revolution

It is difficult to underestimate the importance of *Star Wars* to the movie industry. Not only did it save Twentieth Century Fox, it arguably halted the box-office slide of the seventies. At the time *Star Wars* was released, Fox's stock was selling at $12 a share. Four years later it was $70 a share.

The effect on movies in general was more profound. The popularity of modern cinema had come under a tremendous attack by television. A recent poll of 60,000 people in the UK, sponsored by Sky, of the top 100 movies of the century showed a decided lack of movies from the sixties and seventies. *Star Wars* became a defining moment in restoring large audiences to the cinema screens and, not surprisingly, topped the poll with a massive 35 per cent of the vote. The whole movie industry was revolutionised by *Star Wars*. In the mid-seventies a big movie would open on average on 600 cinema screens. The big movies of today, such as *Godzilla* (1998), now open on 7,000 screens.

Star Wars has been hailed as the touchstone of modern cinema. Adam Bresnick, writing in *The Los Angeles Times*, commented that it 'did more to change Hollywood movies than any film since *The Jazz Singer*. Whereas traditional American cinema largely hewed to the Aristotelian principle that plot and character are the most important elements of a dramatic work, the trilogy is first and foremost about light and spectacle... In keeping with his commitment to spectacle, Lucas changed the structure of the action of the Hollywood feature film. In order to retain the interest of viewers bowled over by the effects, Lucas movies feature what the industry calls "an action beat" every ten minutes.' That may be a little unfair to the story of *Star Wars*, but the spectacle and action of Hollywood feature films do descend from *Star Wars*.

Star Wars also introduced the concept of the event movie. There had been a few 'blockbusters' before *Star Wars*, most notably *Jaws* in 1975, but movies after *Star Wars* were very different. Merchandising, coupled with a summer release date, raised the profile of blockbuster movies and added to the revenue that cinemas brought in.

Science fiction became an important element in many blockbusters. *Star Wars* launched the *Star Trek* and *Alien* series of movies, *Independence Day* (1996), and a whole number of flops including *Flash Gordon* (1980), the rights of which Lucas had originally wanted to buy.

The director Martin Scorsese has commented that the effect of *Star Wars* was twofold. First, it unbalanced movies towards making money rather than art. Second, if you wanted to know the future of the film industry you needed to go to Skywalker Ranch and see George Lucas.

The special-effects revolution

Star Wars was a pioneer of special effects. Lucas saw an integral part of the concept to be cutting-edge technology in producing effects. On such technology Lucas said, 'It means I can make things more believable, and that's important.'[24]

When Lucas began to think about the special effects there were few he could turn to. It had become a rarity in Hollywood. Computer-controlled cameras had been used in the filming of TV commercials, but had not been used to any great extent in a feature film. In July 1975 Lucasfilm Ltd created a subsidiary called Industrial Light and Magic to provide the 350 special effects in *Star Wars*. Lucas appointed John Dykstra to put together a team of young effects wizards. Not only did they have to create the effects, they would also have to build the equipment. Using computer-controlled cameras and computer graphics, Industrial Light and Magic pushed optical effects to the limit.

Industrial Light and Magic, as well as producing the effects and new equipment, also produced the people, at that time many aged in their mid-twenties, who would pave the way for the ground-breaking technology and visual effects of the next two decades. Dykstra and Lucas went their separate ways after *Star Wars*, Dykstra forming his own company and using the crew and equipment to work on Universal's TV series,

Battlestar Galactica. Industrial Light and Magic, relocated by Lucas, became key in many subsequent movies such as *Back to the Future* (1985), *Terminator II* (1991), *Jurassic Park* (1993), *Forrest Gump* (1994) and *Titanic* (1998).

In *Star Wars* special effects and narrative had meshed, a principle which would lie at the foundation of other science-fiction movie series such as *Star Trek* and *Alien*, but also of such terrestrial movies as *Who Framed Roger Rabbit?* (1988), *Backdraft* (1991) and *Twister* (1996).

Special effects provide reality to the imagination. They reinforce a story, allowing people to engage with the characters and situations in a way that relates to our own experience of real things. In the video that accompanies Will Smith's hit record 'Men in Black', an alien joins Smith and dances with him. The realism is a long way from the aliens of the early *Flash Gordon* movies with their fireworks in the back of toy rockets, or even some of the aliens in the original sixties series of *Star Trek*. The special effects encourage you to believe that this can really happen. In fact the special effects were so good in *Star Wars* that they gave Ewan McGregor the impression that speeding across Tatooine on a landspeeder was an everyday occurrence.

The revolution of spirituality

Star Wars unashamedly introduced spirituality into its central themes, exemplified by the Jedi's reliance on the Force. Up to this point, religious films had been in a class of their own and spiritual themes rarely crossed over into main Hollywood features. One of the exceptions was *2001: A Space Odyssey*, made in 1968 by Stanley Kubrick. Lucas thought the technical aspects were great but the movie was too obscure and downbeat. In *Star Wars* Lucas attempted to achieve the same technical excellence within the context of the explicit themes of hope, good and evil, and spirituality.

The influence of this should not be underestimated. It is perhaps best seen in the development of *Star Trek*. Gene Roddenberry, the creator of *Star Trek*, came from a Baptist background but became an atheist and a member of the Humanist Association. The original television series had little at all about spirituality and it seemed to make clear that, in the future, humans would have no need for religion in boldly going about the galaxy.

However, one of the effects of the success of *Star Wars* was to restore confidence in science fiction. This helped *Star Trek* make the transition from television to cinema in a series of movies from 1979 to the present day. As the series developed, so religious themes developed. By *Star Trek III: The Search for Spock* (1984), the cool logic and total reliance on the power of science of the Vulcan Spock is augmented by Vulcan mysticism. In *Star Trek V: The Final Frontier* (1989) a Vulcan prophet leads the crew beyond the frontier of the centre of the galaxy in a search for God. The 'god' they find is simply an alien being in desperate need of a starship. Roddenberry was not happy with the movie. In a letter to his attorney he wrote, 'It would be hard to imagine a more inappropriate time to do a story about a real God or fake God who has mesmerised our usually intelligent and experienced crew into accepting its authenticity.'[25]

Roddenberry was worried about the public's attitude to religion in the light of revelations about television evangelists such as Jim and Tammy Bakker. However, his religious scepticism was in the process of being replaced. The scene with 'god' lasts for six minutes and sharpens the question of whether we make God in our own image.[26]

Yet more sympathetic to religious themes have been the various *Star Trek* spin-off series on television. *Deep Space Nine* centres on a space station near to the planet of Bajor and a nearby wormhole through to a distant part of the galaxy. The Bajorans are deeply religious, with prophets, scriptures, mystics and religious leaders. They are not portrayed as 'primitive' but on the same level of intellect and development as humans and the many other species inhabiting the station. Even Commander Benjamin Sisko becomes involved with the religious beliefs and practices, acting as the religious emissary. Some have pointed to the New Age feel of the series but whatever the religious assumptions, it presents spiritual experience as something that is real and not to be looked down upon in a technological society.

In *Star Trek Voyager*, which began in 1995, Commander Chakotay explores the ancestral spirit world of native North America. Once again, this exists side by side with the technology of the starship and is referred to without it being a sign of weakness; indeed it is very much a strength.

Although this change can be clearly seen in *Star Trek*, it is not alone in science fiction in having a new interest in spirituality. The television series *Babylon 5* views religion and indeed Christianity as an important part of any future society. Its creator, J. Michael Straczynski, explains:

The religious impulse is the flipside of science. Both are attempts to find out where we came from, how we got here, who we are, where we're going. They both use different methodologies, but the impulse is the same. And I use the show to explore the sense of wonder, the exploration, the scientific parts of science fiction and my feeling is 'why not give voice to, or explore the other side as well?' I am an atheist, I have no religious interest personally at all, but as a writer it can lead to some very compelling drama.[27]

Another person fascinated with religion is Chris Carter, creator of The X-Files. He calls himself 'a religious person looking for religious experience'. The X-Files, which premiered on the Fox network in 1993, cleverly takes UFO folklore and puts it into an engaging narrative. David Duchovny's Mulder is the believer contrasted with Gillian Anderson's Scully, who wants scientific proof. Paranormal fascination intermingles with spiritual themes, with the new ingredient of conspiracy theories expressing a mistrust of government and authority structures.

The engagement with spiritual themes is not only in science fiction. The Truman Show (1998) starred Jim Carrey as Truman, the subject of the ultimate fly-on-the-wall documentary. His whole life is artificial: his wife, parents and friends are all actors and his hometown is a massive film set. Truman is the star of a show viewed around the clock by 1.7 billion viewers through 5,000 hidden cameras. It is a very clever satire on television's power and desire to control.

However it is more than that. Time magazine characterised

it as 'a quest movie... [about] our hero's need to know himself and his place in the universe... [about] who's directing our lives? And how do we negotiate with God or fate?' Indeed, in the movie, the creator of 'The Truman Show', Christof, appears as a God character to Truman. Dressed in black and aloof, he shows himself as a control freak serving his own ends at the expense of his creature. Truman eventually escapes by confrontation with his maker. It is a caricature of belief in God. Some see God in the same way – aloof, detached and a control freak.

Titanic, which outperformed *Star Wars* at the US box office, taking $600 million in the US alone, naturally explored death and confidence in human technology. As the character played by Leonardo DiCaprio dies in the freezing water, the song by Céline Dion echoes in the background, 'Near, far, wherever you are – I believe that the heart will go on.' Death and hope, the power and frailty of confidence in human technology, all resonate with our own experiences. They point to the deeper questions in life, such as, How final is death? Why is this world a place of suffering? and Why do we mess up the world?

From the exploration of a future global disaster in *Armageddon* (1998) and *Deep Impact* (1998) to questioning of what is real in *The Matrix* (1999), to the combination of fate and choice explored in *Sliding Doors* (1998), modern cinema has become a focus for the discussion of spirituality, philosophy and theology. Of the films reviewed in a recent book dealing with the relationship of theology and cinema since 1916, nearly 50 per cent were made after *Star Wars*.[28]

Now, of course, many people see movies first and foremost as a source of entertainment, but they can be more than that.

Indeed for many people in their twenties and thirties, who have no link to organised religion, the cinema has become the prime focus of spiritual discussion. Certainly, the nineties have seen an explosion in its popularity. Some intellectuals see it as somewhat vulgar, but that is to underestimate its power to become a vehicle for discussion about the deep questions of life. To this we will return in later chapters.

4

The Phantom Menace and fandom mania

On 1 November 1994 George Lucas took his three adopted children to school and then drove to his office to start work. He wrote by hand with a Ticonderoga No. 2 pencil in a notebook-binder filled with yellow lined paper, the same binder in which he wrote *Star Wars*. It was the beginning of the script for Episode I of the *Star Wars* saga, *The Phantom Menace*.

The plot, which had been in Lucas's mind for some time, had been forced to wait until he was ready. Taking a break from *Star Wars* to do other things in movies and life added to his conviction that he would not create another episode until special effects had developed to a point where they would encompass his imagination.

The effects in movies such as *Jurassic Park* had begun to fulfil the dream, and the special editions of *Star Wars*, *The Empire Strikes Back* and *Return of the Jedi* had allowed Lucas to use new effects on a small scale to improve the original trilogy.

The Phantom Menace was the first film he had directed since 1977. Shooting began on 2 July 1997, and as with *Star Wars* was not without problems. Using Tunisia as the setting for the planet Tatooine meant temperatures of over 50 degrees celsius and a storm which damaged and destroyed everything from buildings on the sets to wigs. Sets had to be rebuilt and painted while actors were on those sets, and 1,400 costumes had to be dug out of the sand and cleaned.

It was not only a big undertaking in terms of sets. The special-effects people and designers would produce three computer-generated worlds in painstaking detail, 140 new aliens and 2,000 computer-generated sequences. The scale of this can be seen by comparison with *Titanic*, which only had 200 sequences.

Fit only for children?

The Phantom Menace had a great deal riding on it. According to *Empire* magazine, the biggest cinema date of 1998 was the launch of the trailer on 17 November. In fact, in many places, this trailer of 125 seconds of film proved to be a bigger box-office draw than the films which accompanied it. In one US cinema, some 500 people paid $9 for *The Siege*, a movie starring Denzel Washington and Bruce Willis. Of those, 300 left before the main feature after having seen *The Phantom Menace* trailer. Some fans would even pay to watch the trailer all day in various cinemas.

When the trailer appeared on the *Star Wars* internet site, the site had 3.5 million hits in the first five days and in the first seven days more than 1.5 million fans downloaded a copy, making it the most frequently accessed video footage ever on the net. Eventually 10 million people would download the trailer. The internet was used by Lucasfilm to advertise *The Phantom Menace* heavily. However, it also became a problem. The film itself became available on the internet after its US opening and could be illegally downloaded in roughly ninety hours. About two months before its UK opening, I went to speak to a group of fifty children about the spirituality of *Star Wars*. At least half of them had already seen *The Phantom Menace* on pirate video!

This proved to be quite a contrast with the original *Star Wars* trailer which in 1977 had to be taken out of some cinemas because it was treated with groans and guffaws, especially when R2-D2 was zapped and fell over.

If the trailer was seen as the biggest cinema event of 1998, the movie itself was called 'the most eagerly awaited movie of the century'. In the US people began queuing in April 1999, some six weeks before the release of the film. Video cameras relayed the queue onto websites and various film crews were there to document the 'line event'. Fans were given the name 'Starwoids' in parallel to *Star Trek*'s 'Trekkies'.

The Phantom Menace opened in the US on 19 May 1999. Fans flew to the US from all parts of the world to get their first viewing of the new story. Opening-day sales were $28.5 million, well beyond the record of $26.1 million set in 1997 by *The Lost World: Jurassic Park*. Approximately $1 million an hour were taken on its opening two days, and by the end of five days $102 million had been taken at the box office. Costing $115 million to make, it was an understatement to say that the movie was going to be profitable!

For months the media on both sides of the Atlantic had been building up the opening, interviewing Lucas and the main stars. The range of new toys had been released bit by bit and the novel and screenplay had been released on 4 May, with the slogan, 'May the fourth be with you.'

On 19 May, the US *Today* programme opened with John Williams' *Star Wars* score and host Katie Couric saying, 'You know it's a cultural phenomenon when we open the show that way.' It is estimated that over 2 million people skipped work on opening day, costing the US economy $300 million in daily production. Only CNN seemed not to want to join in, using the backdrop, '*Star Wars*. Who cares?'

Such an eagerly awaited movie was bound to disappoint some. Early reviews were not terribly favourable. Peter Howell, in *The Toronto Star*, called it 'as overblown as its name', and 'a disappointing example of what happens when Hollywood tries to be all things to all people'. Others characterised it as 'disappointing', 'tired and drained', 'not nearly as satisfying as the originals', and 'fit only for children'. The latter comment may reflect the way that *Star Wars* has expanded beyond its original purpose, that of being a family-orientated movie. Maybe those who saw it first as children want it to speak to them in the same way even though they have grown older.

Others were more enthusiastic. Rogert Ebert called it, 'an astonishing achievement in imaginative film-making' and *USA Today* commented that 'the original *Star Wars* used "humanistic optimism" to soothe American disenchantment sparked by Vietnam and rancour about Watergate. Now a country again tired of petty politics and confused about a war is getting its well-timed refill.'[29] As we shall see in Chapter 8, this latter review is right in identifying optimism as one of the keys to the success of *Star Wars*, but I will suggest that it is far from 'humanistic optimism'.

The fans themselves had different reactions. Rhett Smith, twenty-five years old, said, 'This film wasn't better than sex, but it's right up there in the same league,' while a disappointed Josh Mawkes said, 'It'll make lots of money, but so does the Mafia.'[30]

The boy who would become Vader

John Williams, the composer of the original *Star Wars* theme, explained recently where he got his inspiration for the new music for *The Phantom Menace*. He said, 'I was sitting on the toilet, watching *General Hospital*, when all of a sudden the water gushed and brought together a syncopated harmony perfect for the theme of the boy who will one day become Darth Vader.'[31]

However strange the inspiration, he does sum up the overall plot of Episodes I to III of the *Star Wars* saga. In 1998 a new poster appeared above the studios of Twentieth Century Fox in Century City, Los Angeles. It showed a boy walking alone in a desert casting a shadow immediately recognisable as that of Darth Vader. In one image it encapsulates the development of the story: the corruption of Luke Skywalker's father Anakin and his turn to the dark side of the Force.

Yet Lucas wanted to do other things along the way. The trailer for *The Phantom Menace* opened with the titles:

Every generation has a legend...
Every journey has a first step...
Every saga has a beginning...

In addition to the history of Anakin Skywalker, the history and mythology of the Jedi Knights, their culture and philosophy, the demise of the old Republic, and the rise of Senator Palpatine to the evil Emperor, had to be explored. It allowed Lucas to develop the story already in his mind but only hinted at in the later trilogy.

With the main characters, Lucas's familiar touches are clearly seen. The young, gifted and driven misfit is Anakin Skywalker (played by Jake Lloyd), the young woman is Queen Amidala (played by Natalie Portman), the mystic guide is Jedi Master Qui-Gon Jinn (played by Liam Neeson), the imposing villain is Darth Maul (played by martial-arts expert Ray Park) and the comic sidekick is Jar Jar Binks, this time a computer-generated character rather than a human-operated droid.

Providing continuity with the later trilogy, Ewan McGregor plays a younger Obi-Wan Kenobi, R2-D2 and C-3PO appear, and Ian McDiarmid returns to play Senator Palpatine without the age and evil appearance of the later Emperor.

The opening 'crawl' or scrolling text characteristic of the *Star Wars* series was leaked as early as January 1999 and produced in magazines such as *Vanity Fair* and *Access Hollywood*.

Using the same first line as *Star Wars: A New Hope*, it set the story in the past in 'a galaxy far, far away'. But the context was now very different. A dispute had arisen in the Galactic Republic concerning the taxation of trade routes. The Trade

Federation had blockaded the planet of Naboo and two Jedi Knights had been sent to settle the conflict.

This text sets the scene. To the uninitiated and to many who will have just watched the *Star Wars* movies, it does not set the scene in too much detail. What are the Trade Federation and the Galactic Republic? It is interesting that Lucas does not give much more information. That is partly to draw the viewer in, for it is only in the story that these things begin to emerge.

The basic plot of the rest of the movie is now well known. The two Jedi Knights are Qui-Gon Jinn and his young pupil Obi-Wan Kenobi. Sent to settle the dispute, and helped and hindered by a disaster-prone creature, Jar Jar Binks, who is a Gungan of the planet Naboo, they rescue Amidala the Naboo Queen while the Trade Federation invade. Attempting to take her to the Republic's assembly in Coruscant, their spacecraft's hyperdrive breaks down and they land on Tatooine. Qui-Gon Jinn, whom one critic characterised as looking like a cross between Jesus and a member of Fleetwood Mac, goes to barter for hyperdrive parts with Watto, a hummingbird junk dealer. There he encounters a slave boy, Anakin, in whom he senses a special presence of the Force. Anakin possesses unusual technical ability, agility and perception. Qui-Gon wagers with Watto the freedom of Anakin on the special-effects spectacular set piece, a podrace across the Tatooine desert.

Within this basic plot Lucas has ample space to develop many religious themes. The question of evil is central. Darth Maul, who follows the Jedi Knights across the galaxy in order to frustrate their plans, is a graphic illustration of evil, the red face and horns being a bit of a give-away for such a role! He is apprentice to Darth Sidious, a shadowy figure, whose plan is to use the Trade Federation to take control of the Republic. He is the 'phantom menace' of the title. Together they represent the resurgence of the Sith, an ancient people lured to the dark side, believed by the Jedi to be extinct.

Yet the 'phantom menace' has wider resonances. The question of evil is not just represented by an obvious figure, it is also about how good people become evil.

Senator Palpatine appears to be a good man working for peace at the Republic's assembly. Frustrated by corruption, and critical of the use of bureaucratic power, we see him wanting to replace the current Chancellor Valorum in order to 'bring democracy back to the Republic'. We know Palpatine will end up as the evil Emperor. How does this happen? Is he a well-meaning official and good man wanting to do a good thing who eventually is seduced by power? Or is there something insidious going on? Why is there an invasion of the planet Naboo for which Palpatine happens to be the representative? There are enough clues to fit the picture together that will no doubt be fully revealed in Episodes II and III.

This, however, is secondary to the major question posed through Episodes I to III. How can Anakin Skywalker turn into Darth Vader? How can the precocious innocent boy of Episode I become the evil presence of Episodes IV to VI?

In the story of Anakin many religious themes interweave. As a young child his goodness shows. He 'gives without any thought of reward' and even at this stage is a hero to the other children on Tatooine.[32] The same theme of disrupted family life is seen in Anakin as in Luke. Anakin is a slave with his mother but has to leave her at a young age to become a Jedi. He has no father, and there is the suggestion of a virgin birth.

This parallel with the Christian understanding of Jesus is further developed by the debate which ensues among the Jedi Council, held in the Temple of the Jedi. This is the heyday of the Jedi, when they are the guardians of peace and justice in the galaxy. Qui-Gon believes that Anakin may be the fulfilment of the prophecy which says that one will arise who will bring balance to the Force. Once again, one cannot help hearing echoes of the New Testament referring to Old Testament prophecies concerning the coming of the saviour.

In this debate we learn more about the Force itself. Qui-Gon recognises that the Force is unusually strong with Anakin, and an analysis shows that he has a high concentration of 'midi-chlorians'. This is a microscopic life form that resides in all living cells and communicates with the Force. They are symbionts, speaking of the will of the Force. This makes the Force sound at times quite personal. For example, Qui-Gon states of Anakin, 'finding him was the will of the Force'.[33] The Force does seem to be in providential control: at one point Qui-Gon says to Anakin, 'Our meeting was not a coincidence. Nothing happens by accident.'[34]

Yet at the same time, choice is involved. Anakin can choose to go with Qui-Gon or not, and the Jedi Council debate whether this boy should be allowed to train as a Jedi. The Senior Jedi is Mace Windu (eventually making it from Lucas's initial thirteen-page story into the movies), played by Samuel L. Jackson. The fear is that Anakin is already too old for training as a Jedi. Yoda is worried that there is too much anger in him: 'Fear is the path to the dark side... fear leads to anger... anger leads to hate... hate leads to suffering.'[35] Obi-

Wan questions Qui-Gon's belief in Anakin: 'The boy is dangerous... they all sense it. Why can't you?'[36]

The ground is being prepared for Episodes II and III but already we find ourselves asking, How can Anakin turn to the dark side? The boy will marry Queen Amidala and have two children, Luke and Leia. He will not turn to the dark side until Episode II, but however Lucas is planning to do it, the fundamental question remains. What is it about us that makes us refuse the good? Why are we seduced by power, and can we ever be set free from our bad choices?

To these issues we will return later. One of the features of *The Phantom Menace* has been the marketing of the movie and all its merchandising. It is to that we turn now, to see how important it is to the spirituality of *Star Wars*.

5

May the market force be with you

Every morning my children have breakfast with Anakin Skywalker, with Darth Maul looking directly at them. Darth Vader and a stormtrooper serve them their orange juice, and Luke Skywalker and Leia help them brush their teeth.

This is not fantasy but reality. Their bowls have Anakin during the podrace. The cereal packet has a large picture of Darth Maul. Their cups are modelled on Darth Vader and a stormtrooper. Even their toothbrushes have pictures of Luke and Leia.

My children are five and three years old. Their interest in *Star Wars* is far beyond the fact that Daddy is writing a 'book which does not have any pictures'. *Star Wars* has become a part of their life, even though the three-year-old has never even seen *Star Wars* all the way through. Like the media academic she also falls off to sleep.

Star Wars may have opened up the question of spirituality to modern cinema audiences, but it also had a profound impact on seemingly much more earthly concerns. It gave birth to the most successful merchandising operations ever and transformed the merchandising concept of movies. For example, in 1977 movie merchandising brought in $5 billion in all, but by 1990 this figure had risen to $66 billion.

Up to the launch of *Star Wars*, merchandising had been used to sell movies. After *Star Wars* movies began to sell the merchandise. In fact, the distributor of *Star Wars*, Twentieth Century Fox, had sold a number of lucrative rights to various companies before the film's opening in order to try to promote the film.

Merchandising became big business in itself. The success of the movie and the merchandising revolution is demonstrated in the value that *Star Wars* merchandise has retained and accumulated. For example, a Luke Skywalker figure cost a child 97p when originally purchased. If it is on the card on which it was originally sold it is now worth around £600. Even a Luke figure bought in 1995 can now be worth £200.

The amazing thing about *Star Wars* merchandising is its ability to go beyond the *Star Wars* fanatic. Some collectors do go to extremes, such as Jason Joiner who has 26,000 pieces, the largest selection of *Star Wars* items in the UK. However, *Star Wars* has a much wider appeal. It is estimated that 16 per cent of all US households own *Star Wars* products. According to a promotional brochure from Lucas Licencing, the *Star Wars* product is 'unique in its ability to cross both gender and generational lines'.

Product marking

One of the ways that movies can be promoted and from which big profits can be made is through product marking. That is the licensing of the *Star Wars* logo and characters to be used in advertising or in products. It is something that Lucas has come to see as important, commenting, 'Nabisco sells more crackers than Hollywood sells movie tickets each year.'[37]

The list of products is endless. Over the past twenty years you have been able to buy *Star Wars* T-shirts, monopoly, bubble baths, bed linen, greetings cards, giftwrap, wallpaper, buttons, patches, lunch boxes, belts, jewellery, ceramic mugs, cookie jars, alarm clocks, masks, shoes, slippers, collectables, model kits, chocolates, ice lollies, trading cards and even an R2-D2-shaped swing bin.

Darth Vader promoted Duracell by duelling with an energising bunny, and a Chicago beer was promoted as, 'The best thing out of a can since R2-D2.' Even Disney rides were created from the *Star Wars* story. Such marking shows the appeal of *Star Wars* and its ability to sell.

Games

Industrial Light and Magic is not the only subsidiary of Lucasfilm. LucasArts Entertainment Company has produced some of the best-selling CD-ROM titles of all time, such as *Dark Forces*, *Rebel Assault*, *TIE Fighter* and *Rogue Squadron*. Not only do these games take you into the world of *Star Wars*, but they also expand the story into different characters and situations.

Take a spin in the *Millennium Falcon*, blast stormtroopers or race pods across a desert and you will find yourself in the story. The appeal of these games is not just to children. They have a respectability for teenagers and adults to buy and play.

In all of this, LucasArts has been at the forefront of software design in order to make the games more exciting and realistic.

Toys

The first action figures took a year to appear after *Star Wars*. This reflected both the uncertainty about the popularity of the movie once it was released and the secondary role that merchandising played. However, the demand was so great that Kenner Products sold 'Early Bird' kits, which were empty boxes, with a promise to deliver action figures later.

The demand has never ceased. Toys are now one of the most important aspects of the marketing. In fact, one of the first things to be released in the UK before *The Phantom Menace* movie itself was an action figure, a battle droid on a one-pilot hoverboard. Generations of children (and a few adults) have played with their models of the *Millennium Falcon*, fought with plastic lightsabres and bought action figures of obscure characters because Luke, Leia and Han have been all sold out.

Some of the toys are quite bizarre. In a recent catalogue of *Star Wars* toys, a mask of Admiral Ackbar's face and even his hands was advertised. The mind boggles: Who would want such things?

Publishing

When Bantam published *Heir to the Empire* by Timothy Zahn in 1991 there was little idea whether a *Star Wars* novel that went beyond the movies would work. Yet it went to the top of *The New York Times* hardcover bestsellers' list and spawned yet another successful branch of merchandising. *Star Wars* books, including titles such as *The Courtship of Princess Leia*, have sold over a million copies in the UK in the last few years, and have constantly been in the US fiction bestseller list. In addition to these books there have been graphic novels, comics and syndicated comic strips.

Behind these books was a carefully managed strategy. George Lucas wanted to explore stories about the era after *Return of the Jedi*. He carefully manages the *Star Wars* story so that plot and character are consistent with the original trilogy. For example the story of Jedi Master Yoda is carefully guarded in order to retain the mystery of the character.

It is not only the novels that have produced publishing success. Books which tell the story and trivia behind the making of the film and 'technical' books exploring the interior of spaceships and character backgrounds are also extremely popular.

Why merchandising?

Why is merchandising so important to the success of *Star Wars*? At one level every part of an empire is a marketing device for the rest. The movies encourage people to buy the toys and the toys encourage people to see the movies. At the next level, merchandising is used as a financial foundation for Lucas's independence and the development of his company's interests. When you realise that new toys released from *The*

Phantom Menace are expected to make more than $1 billion, that Pepsi paid $2 billion for the *Star Wars* licence to mark its drinks and to be used by KFC, Taco Bell and Pizza Hut, and that Sony Classical will release more than a million copies of the soundtrack by John Williams, then it is clear there is plenty of money to fund new movies, Skywalker Ranch and many other things in the Lucas empire. In fact *The Phantom Menace* cost an estimated $115 million, but Hasbro alone paid $100 million for the film's toy licences.

However, the merchandising works on an even deeper level. It develops the myth. When I was a student in the early eighties one of the highlights of college life was when a *Star Wars* arcade game was installed in the bar. Computer games then were very basic by today's standards in graphics and variety, but each evening, lunchtime, and any other time that was free, it would be surrounded by a small group of people.

For a small fee you could become Luke Skywalker on a mission to blow up the Death Star. First, you had to take on a number of TIE fighters who would shoot vast fuzzy electronic snowballs at you. Having blasted them, you would hear the machine say, 'We're going in,' and you would see on the screen in front of you the famous trench on the surface of the Death Star on the way to the exhaust port that you had to hit. Trying to avoid the walls and the bridges in the trench, which because of the lack of computing power were transparent, was not easy but just possible. As you fired into the port you heard Obi-Wan Kenobi say, 'Trust the Force.' Then your X-wing fighter would be whisked away to see the Death Star explode. The only trouble was that success did not mean a hug from Princess

Leia, but simply that you would have to do it all again. This time the TIE fighters had more strange snowballs, and there were more bridges in the trench, and so on, and so on.

Even with the lousy graphics and repetitive plot, we would all get into the game. As you tried to dodge the snowballs and the bridges, you would sway your body left to right, and up and down, to somehow encourage your spacecraft to survive. Having exploded the Death Star you would release the controls and stand back a fraction with an air of achievement and a need for others to recognise your power of the Force.

The game was involving you in the *Star Wars* story and developing its concept. As the merchandising has gone from fuzzy snowballs to the amazing graphics of podracing in the desert of Tatooine, so its potential to do the same thing has grown. How does it do this?

First, it stimulates the imagination. Lucas comments, 'one of the things I like about *Star Wars* is that it stimulates the imagination, and that's why I don't have any qualms about the toys or about any of the things that are going on around *Star Wars*, because it does allow young people to use their imagination'.[38] The child playing with the action figure, the teenager with the computer game or the adult reading the novel are engaging their imagination. They are asking the questions, What would it be like to be part of this? and What is this universe like?

Second, it gives reality to the imagination. Richard Marquand, the producer of *Return of the Jedi*, said, 'One of the reasons that *Star Wars* is so terrific is because it is absolutely real... and it's drummed into everybody. Whether it involves Chewbacca or Jabba the Hutt – it has, above all, to be real.

Real relationships and real action that stem from real emotions.'[39]

It is fascinating that a story of science fantasy tries so hard to be real. Yet imagination can only be stimulated if it has some basis or connection to the everyday world. In addition, the all-pervasive *Star Wars* marketing subtly puts the story into eating, drinking, sleeping and play. Qui-Gon Jinn may wander the galaxy to bring peace and justice, but he is also on the back of my Pepsi can!

The design of *Star Wars* reinforces reality. Lucas, to a large extent, takes designs from historical cultures to create the 'new' worlds of his galaxy. In the filming of *Star Wars* he insisted that sets, droids and clothing looked grubby and old rather than shiny and new. This gave the impression of age and of a real world.

As we saw earlier, special effects also give a sense of these things really happening. The superiority of the graphics on the recent CD-ROM game, *Star Wars Episode I: The Phantom Menace*, over my college *Star Wars* machine reinforces that reality. The growth industry in the 'technical' books of *Star Wars*, showing in great detail the inner workings of everything from lightsabres to X-wing fighters, reflects this also. For example, a schematic of a Republic cruiser which makes a brief appearance in *The Phantom Menace*, ferrying the two Jedi Knights to the planet Naboo, shows anyone who is interested that:

- its red colour means it comes in peace
- it can accommodate a crew of eight plus sixteen passengers

- it is 380 ft long
- it has already seen thirty-four years of diplomatic service
- its engines consist of radiation dampers, magnetic turbines, cooling shrouds, a fuel atomiser cone and an ion-generator ring
- the Captain's quarters are next to the formal dining room.

Why are people interested in this? Perhaps people want the reality because they want to trust the story.

Third, the merchandising encourages involvement. Liam Neeson said that, in the first scene that he and Ewan McGregor were in, 'We kept laughing and shouting, "Yeah! We're in *Star Wars*!"'[40] In fact, it is said that McGregor had a tendency to produce his own sound effects while duelling with a lightsabre, honed from years of practice as a child! The games and the toys allow you to become personally involved in the story. Interactive games bring the player into the process. You can decide what to do, you can be part of the larger concept and you can determine the outcome. The merchandising takes the movie beyond a spectator event. It involves you in ownership of the concept and in a community of others who also find it exciting.

So merchandising communicates the concept and brings reality to the mythology. Lucas commented, 'I took over control of the merchandising not because I thought it was going to make me rich, but because I wanted to control it. I wanted to make a stand for social, safety and quality reasons. I didn't want someone using the name *Star Wars* on a piece of junk.'[41] That is borne out by the high quality of product that comes out of LucasArts or the many licences.

However, there are two other reasons why he wanted to be in control. The merchandising has not made him excessively rich, but it has funded his companies and independence. He also wanted to be in control because he is almost obsessionally protective of the mythology of *Star Wars*. He created it and it means an enormous amount to him. It is to that we turn next.

6

'Every generation has a legend...'

George Lucas has created a legend and indeed is himself a legend to many people. He is an unassuming man who believes passionately in what he does. He was born in 1944 in the small town of Modesto, California.

In 1982 Lucasfilm Ltd invited its employees to a Fourth of July picnic. A company yearbook was circulated with the following seventy-three-word biography of Lucas:[42]

GEORGE LUCAS: Chairman of the Board
HOMETOWN: Off Hwy 99
FAMILY: Growing
SCHOOLS: Downey High, Modesto Junior College, University of Southern California
INTEREST: CBS Evening News, *Sixty Minutes*
SIGN: Taurus
EMPLOYMENT HISTORY: 1966 turned down at Hanna Barbera Productions, 1967 turned down at Cornell

Wilde Productions, 1968 first script rejected by United Artists (*THX 1138*), 1969 second script rejected by every major and minor studio (*American Graffiti*), 1981 went into business for myself.

Such a brief history is characteristically self-effacing, but hides a fascinating story of movies and spirituality. Indeed, to understand fully the *Star Wars* movies of George Lucas you need to understand a little about the man.

God, Flash and crash

Lucas was the son of a hard-working, successful businessman. Comic books and cliffhanger serials such as *Adventure Theatre* on an early television set were two of his earliest interests. *Flash Gordon* was a particular favourite. It is said that his idea of heaven as a child would be a box of biscuits and a pile of comics. The attractive graphics and simple messages of the comics would have a deep effect on him and surface again in *Star Wars*. Indeed during his writing of *Star Wars* he would go and buy comics 'to get into the mind of a ten-year-old'.

His religious background was varied. When he was six years old, he had some kind of mystical experience. He later described it as, 'It centred around God, what is God, but more than that, what is reality? What is this? It's as if you reach a point and suddenly you say, "Wait a second, what is the world? Where are we? What am I? How do I function in this, and what's going on here?"'[43]

His parents went to a Methodist church but he disliked

what he saw as self-centred religion and resented Sunday school. However, his housekeeper would take him with her to the German Lutheran church, where he liked the ritual. Lucas commented, 'I think church is a much better experience than Sunday school because it gets into what religion is all about; the ceremony provides something essential for people.'[44] As with the comics, some of these early experiences would appear later in *Star Wars*.

He loved the family's regular trips to Disneyland. There the imagination could be stimulated, and you could become part of the movies. As he grew as a teenager, he began to lack direction in life. Perhaps fearful of being submerged in his father's business he looked for thrills in car racing and began to slip in his grades at school.

Then in 1962 something happened which had a profound effect on him. On a corner into the road towards his home, his car overturned and wrapped itself around a tree. Unexpectedly, the seat belt broke, throwing Lucas clear of the car and certain death. In hospital he began to rethink his direction in life. He said, 'You can't have that kind of experience and not feel there must be a reason why you're here. I realised I should be spending my time trying to figure out what that reason is and trying to fulfil it.'[45]

The effect of the car crash is sometimes overstated. Dale Pollock's unauthorised biography of Lucas puts the crash at the start of the account of his life, as if everything flowed from there.[46] This is perhaps exaggerating its significance. It was a significant moment in the life and thought of George Lucas, as it would have been for all of us, but there were many more influences as well.

From cynicism to optimism

This new direction meant that Lucas studied anthropology, philosophy and sociology, and then enrolled in the University of Southern California film school. There his senior film, *Freiheit*, explored the concept of freedom in the escape of a man from East to West Germany. Another student film, *1:42:08*, made in 1966, expressed his love of car racing. This love of car racing would surface again in the sequence of the speeder bikes in the forests of Endor in *Return of the Jedi* and in the podracing sequence in *The Phantom Menace*.

Having failed the draft for Vietnam on medical grounds, he continued with film-making. Assisting as part of a training programme for Navy film-makers he made *THX 1138:4EB* in 1967. This picked up again the theme of freedom, this time telling the story of an individual's escape from a mechanistic and dehumanised future. It was mainly shot in underground car parks and became the winner at the Third National Student Film Festival.

THX 1138:4EB established Lucas's reputation as an imaginative and new breed of film-maker. On the strength of it he made another short film, *6-18-67*, during the filming of the western adventure *McKenna's Gold* (1969), and then made a documentary of the making of *The Rain People* (1968), a film directed by the rising star of Hollywood, Francis Coppola. With Coppola, and a number of other young film-makers, he formed American Zoetrope, the vision being to set up a film community of young under-thirties who would provide an alternative to the Hollywood studios where very few, whether directors or technicians, were under the age of fifty.

With encouragement from Coppola, he rewrote *THX 1138:4EB* as a feature film for Warner Bros. At twenty-three years old, Lucas was about to make his first major movie. He used the half-completed tunnels for the new San Francisco transit system as a set. The movie developed the student version, with the main character, THX 1138, living in an underground world controlled by computers, and sedated by drugs. People are all alike, sex is eliminated by the drugs and the police are robots. Evading their drugs, THX 1138 and his room-mate have sex, conceive a child and eventually THX 1138 escapes to a new world. Already some of the proto-ideas in *Star Wars* are there: the tussle between technology and the human spirit, plus individual action in the face of a repressive system.

When *THX 1138* was delivered to Warner Bros, they did not like it. They took the movie away from Lucas and gave it to one of their inhouse editors. In addition, Warner Bros cancelled a multi-movie deal with Zoetrope on the basis of their dislike of Lucas's movie. Lucas was devastated. He resented the way that the movie had been taken out of his control and felt responsible for the negative effect on Zoetrope. *THX 1138* was eventually released, but failed to break even at the box office.

This was a foundational experience in Lucas's view of the big Hollywood studios. He resented their control and longed for independence and control of his own product. It also saw a change from pessimism to hope in his movies. If he was going to reach audiences and change anything, the stories couldn't be about how bad things were, they had to be about how good things could be.

Following this experience, Lucas got to know Gary Kurtz who had served for four years in a marine photography unit in Vietnam. Kurtz was a Quaker and the horror of the war had forced a spiritual awakening. They wondered whether they should make *Apocalypse Now*, a story that Lucas and John Milius had discussed in college and had begun before *THX 1138*. Of course *Apocalypse Now* (1979) would be later made by Coppola.

However, Lucas was wanting to make more positive films. Lucas told the *Los Angeles Times* in 1973, 'You can learn from cynicism, but you can't build on it.'[47] Both he and Kurtz were fascinated by the *Flash Gordon* serials they had watched as children, and Lucas wanted to make a similar kind of space movie. They tried to buy the movie rights to the Flash Gordon books by Alex Raymond, but Italian director Federico Fellini had got there first.

Lucas was disappointed, but another idea was beginning to form. He began to think about making his own space movie. In the meantime, his immediate plan was to make a movie about rock and roll. He co-wrote and directed *American Graffiti* (1973) which was produced by Coppola. The story was about what it means to be a teenager, chasing girls and having fun. Largely taken from Lucas's own experience it was about teenagers breaking out of their backgrounds, a theme which Luke Skywalker would resurrect some four years later.

Yet again Lucas was looking to make a positive film. Speaking at the Modesto Rotary Club about *American Graffiti* in 1973 he said, 'I decided it was time to make a movie where people felt better coming out of the theatre than when they went in. It had become depressing to go to the movies.'[48]

Eventually, after virtually everyone else had rejected the idea, Universal agreed to finance and distribute it and it turned into a huge success. It became one of the twenty most profitable pictures of all time, costing $775,000 to make but selling $117 million in tickets. It also spurred a flood of nostalgia. One of the film's actors, Ron Howard, went on to star in the television series *Happy Days*, which romanticised the US of the fifties and sixties. Other nostalgia movies, such as the hugely successful *Grease* (1978), owe their origin to *American Graffiti*.

The crisis of the seventies

All of these experiences, successes and failures were being reflected in Lucas's 'space movie'. With the success of *American Graffiti*, Lucas had gained a greater reputation and some money. Now was the time to move forward on it. Before we come to the specific ingredients that would go into the movies that would become the *Star Wars* saga, it is worth noting the historical and cultural background in which it was written and conceived. The mid-seventies was not an optimistic time for the developed world and in particular for the US.

The oil crisis

The rise in OPEC oil prices had a profound effect on the Western nations and sent the US economy into steep decline. The march of technology began to stutter because the fuel that powered it began to cost too much. The utopia of bigger and cheaper cars, better air-conditioning and consumer heaven, though not shattered, was severely dented.

Ecology

The publication of Rachel Carson's *The Silent Spring* in 1965 heralded the beginning of ecological concern that our technological progress was actually messing up the planet. Concern was not as widespread or as informed as it became in the eighties, but people began to notice the way we were depleting mineral resources and polluting the atmosphere – not least in the smog of Los Angeles.

The Vietnam War

In 1975 US troops withdrew from South Vietnam after bloody defeat. For all its power and technology, the US could not destroy the guerrilla fighters in North Vietnam and Cambodia. Those who fought in the hell were welcomed back not as heroes, but as an embarrassment to a nation that wanted to forget the mess it had made.

The Cold War

It is difficult now, with the knowledge of the collapse of communism and the progress in nuclear disarmament, to fully understand how the threat of nuclear destruction loomed large in Western thought, or why the Iron Curtain seemed so immovable. But this was the decade that was to lead to Ronald Reagan's 'star wars' initiative of satellite lasers and vehement anti-nuclear protests. Here was a world able through technology to land missiles thousands of miles away, yet unable to discuss issues amicably. Here was a world struggling with conflicting ideas about freedom and progress. Did capitalism or communism provide freedom for all, or was freedom an illusion?

Watergate

When Richard Nixon resigned following an investigation into the bugging of the Democratic headquarters, it marked a growing distrust of politicians and indeed the political process itself. Authority was corrupted and corrupting. If the dream of technological progress was going to be managed or directed, who would be up to such a thing?

The stalling of the space programme

On 20 July 1969, Michael Collins, Neil Armstrong and Buzz Aldrin gave the US victory in the space race and huge national pride in their 'one small step' to the Moon. They achieved the goal set by President John F. Kennedy in 1961, to land a man on the Moon and return him safely to Earth before the end of the decade. It was a most remarkable achievement and demonstrated the power of technology. Here was America conquering yet another frontier, and it made it all the better that they did it before the Russians.

Dreams were big. This was only one small step in the exploration of the universe. But as the public became bored with moon rock, and the funding was cut, humans did not make a further step. We began to see just how big that frontier of space really was and how it would not be conquered within many lifetimes. The ending of the Apollo missions was yet another disappointment for the progress of technology.

The decline of religion

The sixties had questioned traditional religious teaching about belief and lifestyle. In the seventies, surveys in the US showed that 95 per cent of people believed in God, but only 43 per cent attended church. Scientific advances had questioned God as creator of the universe, the sexual revolution had turned on its head traditional moral teaching, and increasing prosperity was laying the foundations of the greedy capitalism of the late seventies and early eighties. Were the ancient myths of religion relevant any more to the modern world?

It was in this context that Lucas launched *Star Wars*.

7

'You've got something jammed in here real good'

The movie that became *Star Wars* had a number of important components 'jammed into it', in addition to Lucas's own history and the general historical context in which he created it. He said of his desire:

> I wanted to do a modern fairy tale – a myth. One of the things that occurred to me was that I had seen the western movie die. We hardly knew what had happened – one day we turned around and there just weren't any westerns anymore... I wanted to make a space fantasy more in the genre of Edgar Rice Burroughs... I looked at lots of movies – all kinds. Everything: *Flash Gordon*, spy movies, westerns, samurai movies, Errol Flynn movies, space movies, science-fiction movies.[49]

The power of myth

Lucas was an anthropologist before he switched to film studies. He had long had a fascination with the great stories of human existence. Technically called 'myths', these were stories which, within a particular culture, explained the world in which that culture lived, imagined a better world, and probed questions of origin, purpose and value. Myths posed questions such as, Is there more to life than this? Is there more to the world than this? Is there a God or gods and what is the nature of god? What is our relationship with god? and What has gone wrong with the world?

For example, whatever the historical status of the early chapters of the book of Genesis in the Bible, all Old Testament scholars would agree that the story of Adam and Eve addresses these fundamental questions. It claims that there is one God who is creator of the whole universe, that he wants a relationship of intimacy in the context of which he gives human beings responsibility to look after the world, and that things have gone wrong with the world because we have refused to obey God. To say that this story is a myth in this sense is not to say that it is untrue or historically inaccurate, but to recognise that it deals with these fundamental questions of human existence.

As he began to put the ideas for his space movie together, Lucas went to classic books on mythology: 'I sat down over a period of two years and wrote the screenplay. I did a lot of research, mostly in the area of mythology. I studied folktales and people like Bruno Bettelheim and Joseph Campbell, who were writing about mythology.'[50]

Joseph Campbell, in his book *The Hero with a Thousand Faces*, looks at the myths of different cultures and times and suggests that in fact they only offer a limited number of responses to the questions of life. He recognises that, 'Throughout the inhabited world, in all times and under every circumstance, the myths... have flourished; and they have been the living inspiration of whatever else may have appeared out of the activities of the human body and mind.'[51]

Campbell argues that all the stories draw on a common store of images and symbols. In this he was influenced by Carl Jung and the concept of archetypes. That is, certain psychological urges and instincts manifest themselves in fantasies and reveal their presence in symbolic motifs and characters. Central to this, Campbell suggests that the archetype of the hero is the archetype of all human myth. Characters such as knights, dragons or wizards help or hinder the hero on the path to enlightenment. In the stories that speak to us most deeply, Campbell argues that these elements are remarkably constant.

Lucas drew a great deal on Joseph Campbell, both he and Gary Kurtz becoming fascinated with the idea of archetypes. The admiration was mutual. After the success of *Star Wars*, Campbell himself became interested in the mythology of the saga, participating in a series of conversations with journalist Bill Moyers which was filmed at Lucas's Skywalker Ranch and became the book, *The Power of Myth*.[52]

Bruno Bettelheim was Professor of Psychology and Psychiatry at the University of Chicago. During the Second World War he was interned in the concentration camps of Dachau and Buchenwald. In that experience he began to analyse behaviour in order to keep alive and remain human. This concern with how we keep our humanity in the face of the brutalising tendencies inherent in all mass societies, in particular the effect on children, led among other things to a study of fairy tales. From Sinbad to Cinderella he showed how the content of such stories was used by children to help them cope with baffling emotions, helplessness and mystery.[53]

As one of Lucas's biographers comments, 'What the myths revealed to Lucas, among other things, was the capacity of the human imagination to conceive alternate [sic] realities to cope with reality: figures and places and events that were before now or beyond now but were rich with meaning to our present.'[54] They also reminded Lucas that we are all asking similar questions.

In asking those questions and struggling for answers people can be changed. Joseph Campbell highlighted this point when he said, 'What all the myths have to deal with is transformations of consciousness of one kind or another. You have been thinking one way, you now have to think a different way.'[55] That was what Lucas wanted to do. In particular, he had a concern for young people and the kind of belief and moral responsibility that they were being influenced to take up. He said, 'I was trying to make a modern mythology where you take the values and social mores that exist today and put them in a form that you can express to younger people.'[56]

By creating his own new myth of Star Wars, Lucas was avoiding the temptation to preach to the audience. A myth captures themes of timeless value, but does so in a way that relates to the time it is told. He could express concern about society, morals and religion in the contemporary US, but by doing it in story, and keying into these timeless values, the concern would resonate in cultures all over the world. He later spoke about the further value of myths: 'Myths tell us these old stories in a way that doesn't threaten us. They're in an imaginary land where you can be safe. But they deal with real truths that need to be told. Sometimes the truths are so painful that stories are the only way you can get through to them psychologically.'[57]

Swords and princesses

If some of the myths, such as King Arthur and the Knights of the Round Table, were about swords and princesses, Lucas found a contemporary cinematic version in the work of Akira Kurosawa. Born in 1910, his classic *Seven Samurai* (1954) had inspired the western, *The Magnificent Seven* (1960). But in his samurai adventure fantasy, *The Hidden Fortress* (1958), Lucas found a story about a young stroppy princess and a loyal general making a hazardous journey across wild enemy territory – complete with royal treasure, two bumbling companions, helmeted warriors, swords and graphic action. The swords became lightsabres, the samurai became Jedi and the two bumbling companions became robots.

Lucas was impressed that Kurosawa told the story of *The Hidden Fortress* from the point of view of the two companions, who were serfs. The concept of telling the story from the point of view of the 'lowest' characters raised the profile of C-3PO and R2-D2 in the *Star Wars* saga.

The sword fighting also linked in with the Errol Flynn

movies, such as *The Adventures of Robin Hood* (1938), which had represented the high point of the Hollywood swashbuckler. These movies had died out in Hollywood but captured a sense of adventure and romance.

Yet Kurosawa had a more subtle influence on Lucas: 'I found it very interesting that nothing was explained. You are thrown into this world, and obviously if you know about feudal Japan then it makes sense to you; but if you don't, it's like you're watching this very exotic, strange thing with strange customs and a strange look. And I think that influenced me a great deal in working in science fiction because I was able to get around the idea that you have to explain everything or understand what everything is.'[58] It is a characteristic of the *Star Wars* series that everything is not fully explained 'up front'.

Superheroes in outer space

Lucas loved comics and the old adventure serials he had watched as a boy. Having tried unsuccessfully to buy the rights to Flash Gordon, he realised that he could create 'a character as easily as Alex Raymond, who took his character from Edgar Rice Burroughs. It's your basic superhero in outer space.'[59]

Alongside his reading in the area of myth, he read a range of science fiction, from Alex Raymond and Edgar Rice Burroughs to Frank Herbert and E.E. 'Doc' Smith. Comic strips such as *Flash Gordon* and *Buck Rogers* in the 1930s, and their serialisation on television or in the movies, contributed a great deal to the story, look and feel of *Star Wars*.

The traditional motifs of science fiction – a variety of aliens and supernatural powers – were mixed with art-deco sets, blaster guns, video screens, medieval costumes and constant action. The scrolled introductions of the 'story so far' were transplanted from *Flash Gordon* to *Star Wars*. Lucas was also inspired by Fritz Lang's *Metropolis* (1926): C-3PO was inspired by Rothwang's robot.

These are some of the obvious borrowings which have been identified by many reviewers, and by Lucas himself. However, once again, more subtle influences were also at work. The science-fiction writer Brian Aldiss, noting a number of elements essential to 'space opera', points out that one in particular is that 'all must come right in the end'.[60] Even the cliffhanger serial has to have a resolution to it eventually, and that resolution has to be good. Flash Gordon has to save the world (and Dale Arden) from Ming the Merciless at some point.

This sense of 'good closure' to the story was foundational to the concept of hope in *Star Wars*.

Gunslingers on the frontier

After the Second World War, Hollywood enjoyed the golden age of the western. John Ford's *Fort Apache* (1948), *She Wore a Yellow Ribbon* (1949) and *Rio Grande* (1950) pictured heroes conquering the frontier of the Wild West. They were hugely successful movies and within them 'subjects like race relations, sexuality, psychoanalysis and Cold War politics were explored in an imaginative way'.[61] Set in the past, they had the quality of myth – they allowed people to think about the issues in a non-threatening way, and affirmed America's past successes.

However, by the seventies, the western in the classic sense had disappeared. Popular TV shows such as *The Lone Ranger*, *The Virginian*, *Bonanza* and *The High Chapperal* had displaced the need for Hollywood features, and the spaghetti westerns of Sergio Leone such as *The Good, the Bad and the Ugly* (1966) had taken the western in a completely different direction. In addition, attitudes to native North Americans were beginning to change, and the traditional 'good cowboys against evil Indians' structure was falling apart.

Lucas stated, 'At college, one of my instructors said that the western was the last of the American mythology and probably one of the last of the world mythologies developed. Then in the sixties, the western sort of fell by the wayside, especially in the film business… One of the reasons I started doing the film was that I was interested in creating a new kind of myth and using space to do it, because that's the new frontier.'[62]

The western provided many motifs for *Star Wars*. For instance, life on the frontier is represented by Luke's life with Uncle Owen and Aunt Beru. As farmers on the edge of civilisation they employ droids as 'cattlehands' and face all the challenges of an untamed frontier. In fact, when the stormtroopers kill his uncle and aunt, Luke's burning homestead is very reminiscent of a similar scene from John Wayne's *The Searchers* (1956). Blasters are in holsters on the hip in deliberate imitation of western gunfighters, Han Solo is a 'gun for hire' and the cantina in the space port of Mos Eisley could be any bar or saloon of a frontier town – apart, of course, from the extra aliens!

Star Wars replaced the western mythology. Able to ask the same questions of myth, the motifs of the western no doubt keyed into US nostalgia about life and success on the frontier.

A mysterious land to explore

If the old frontier of the Wild West could no longer be explored, Lucas was clear what the new frontier was. He said, 'We were just beginning the Space Age, and it was all very alluring to say, gee, we could build a modern mythology out of this mysterious land that we're about to explore.'[63]

Putting this a slightly different way, he commented, 'One of the reasons I started doing the film was that I was interested in creating a new kind of myth and using space to do it because that's the new frontier.'[64]

By the time that *Star Wars* was being made, as we have seen, the new frontier was becoming less of a priority to explore. Nevertheless, space became an essential ingredient of *Star Wars*. Why was it so important? A story in which spaceships figured so largely did remind people of the huge achievement of the Apollo landings and the triumph over the Russians. The story of travel between the stars and discovering new aliens and planets allowed the longing of many, fed by the early space achievements yet frustrated by the stalling of the space programme, to be expressed. Finally, space encourages wonder. Even if Apollo was no longer blasting into space, new telescopes and probes such as the Voyager spacecraft, which would explore the outer planets and then begin the journey beyond our own solar system, encouraged a sense of wonder at the universe: How big is the universe? What is the significance of human beings in all of this, and is there other life out there? The 'mysterious land' of Star Wars, in keying into this sense of wonder, was important for its success.

Mystery and guidance

After the success of Star Wars representatives from virtually all the world's religious communities at some point claimed that Star Wars was a good expression of their own faith. Certainly there are elements of Buddhism, particularly in Yoda in The Empire Strikes Back. However, Lucas was writing within a Western culture predominantly shaped by the Judeo-Christian culture and out of his own upbringing within Christianity.

Allegories of myth and religion do lie behind many stories of science fiction and fantasy. For example C.S. Lewis' orthodox Christianity is expressed in his fantasy Narnia stories and in his science-fiction stories.

Some have argued that, like the Narnia series, Star Wars reflects something of the Christian story allegorically. When Universal's Battlestar Galactica (1978) appeared the following year, it was inundated with lawsuits claiming that it had been copied directly from Star Wars. As we have seen, the fact that many of the team who worked on Star Wars also worked on Battlestar Galactica meant that the two movies had many similarities. Yet its creator Glen Larson claimed in defence to have lifted the plot, not from Star Wars, but straight from the Bible, without the need of intermediaries!

Star Wars is not a Christian allegory, but it does use a

number of Christian motifs to explore concepts of mystery and guidance. The journalist Bill Moyers, in a recent interview with Lucas, suggested that Star Wars reflected the biblical themes of fall, wandering, redemption and return. He also drew a parallel between Satan tempting Christ by offering him the kingdoms of the world and Vader tempting Luke to come and rule the galaxy with him.[65]

Others have gone further and suggested somewhat tenuous links with biblical events. When Alderaan is destroyed by the Death Star in Star Wars: A New Hope, Obi-Wan Kenobi feels a terrible disturbance in the Force. Some have likened this to Jesus feeling the power drain out of him when he healed a woman who touched his cloak in the midst of a crowd.

Of course you can argue for coincidences in the story of Star Wars in terms of particular incidents, but what is far more important is the underlying philosophy. In the interview with Moyers, Lucas denies that Star Wars is 'religion for the masses without commitment' but acknowledges that the core issues of Star Wars, such as friendship and loyalty, redemption and hope, and the struggle of good versus evil, owe a great deal to Christianity.

Lucas does not mention God explicitly in Star Wars. However, the Force poses the same type of question: Is there more to the universe than just the material? The notion of the Force came from the story in Carlos Casteneda's Tales of Power, in which the Native American shaman Don Juan talks of a 'life force'. As we will see in a later chapter, Lucas takes it over to explore the nature of transcendence and what it means to hope. By transcendence, I mean a reality beyond this physical universe.

Many believe that Lucas has created a myth or sacred story to express religious themes. In conversation, this time with Joseph Campbell, Bill Moyers points out, 'It wasn't just the production value that made such an exciting film to watch, it was that it came along at a time when people needed to see in recognisable images the clash of good and evil. They needed to be reminded of idealism, to see a romance based on selflessness rather than selfishness.'[66]

Emile Durkheim, the prime mover of the sociological way of viewing religion in terms of its function, argued that religion provides an individual with inner strength, purpose, meaning and a sense of belonging. On myths he said, 'Beliefs, myths, dogmas and legends are... representations which express the nature of sacred things.'[67] Lucas in the myth of *Star Wars* is trying to do exactly that. His 'sacred things' are values such as self-sacrifice, nobility and valour, and ideas of mystery and guidance. Mary Henderson concludes her book *Star Wars: The Magic of Myth* by pointing out that *Star Wars* 'fulfils the basic function of myth: to open our hearts to the dimension of mystery in our lives and to give us some guidance on our own hero's journey'.[68]

That Lucas does this without tying *Star Wars* to any particular religion, but uses story and the Force in a very general sense, gives *Star Wars* accessibility to people of many different religious faiths and none. Underneath are Lucas's own beliefs and commitments. As Dale Pollock writes, 'Hard work, self-sacrifice, friendship, loyalty, and a commitment to a higher purpose: these are the tenets of Lucas's faith.'[69]

Lucas is very explicit in acknowledging the importance of this, 'I mean, there's a reason this film is so popular. It's not that I'm giving out propaganda nobody wants to hear.'[70]

We do need to be careful, however, not to characterise the story of *Star Wars* as a carefully crafted piece of religious manipulation. In the writing process itself Lucas confesses, 'I was trying to take certain mythological principles and apply them to a story. Ultimately, I had to abandon that and just simply write the story. I found that when I went back and read it, then started applying it against the sort of principles that I was trying to work with originally, they were all there.'[71] The good story naturally contained these elements of myth.

Ice cream at the movies

Lucas was creating a new myth, but his particular contribution was to tell his story through cinema to a generation whose primary means of interpreting the world and explaining behaviour is no longer religion or literature but film. Orville Schell, Dean of the School of Journalism at the University of California, characterises Lucas as 'a kind of king consolidator of mythology. By blending and reprocessing elements from Homer, Jason, Jesus, King Arthur, Siegfried and Huck Finn with the Viking sagas, the Brothers Grimm, Hans Christian Anderson, Flash Gordon movies and Tolkien's fantasies into a new all-purpose amalgamation, Lucas created... a new "journey of the hero".'[72] Each of these elements speaks of a different world. They are amplified by the power of film to stimulate and give reality to the imagination. Lucas expressed his love of film as, 'It takes all the aspects of other art forms – painting, music, literature, theatre – and puts them into one art form. It's a combination of all these, and it works on all the senses. For that reason it's a very alluring, kind of dreamlike experience. You sit in a very dark room and have this other world come at you in a very realistic way.'[73]

Film is also a truly international art form. 'I was amazed at how the film was accepted all over the world,' Lucas said recently, 'That, more than anything else, was very revealing of the way that popular culture seems to get everywhere you can possibly imagine on this planet.'[74] I suggest that this is not just about how popular culture is accepted, but also how cleverly Lucas has used universal spiritual themes in *Star Wars*.

At a family meal recently we shared together a huge ice-cream sundae of different flavours of ice cream, fruit, nuts, chocolate, fudge brownies and biscuits. It is an image that Lucas frequently uses of *Star Wars*, saying, 'There is a lot taken from western, mythology and samurai movies. It's all the things that are great put together. It's not like one kind of ice cream but rather a very big sundae.'[75] But a sundae only works if there is something holding it all together. The glass dish in which it is contained is essential to the whole experience! However, it may not be immediately noticed and is not as exciting as the ice cream or the brownies.

This is what the spiritual themes do for *Star Wars*. They may not be immediately noticeable, but they are there and they are crucially important. They hold together the mythical elements, the swords and princesses, the gunslingers, the superheroes in outer space and the new frontier of space. It is to these themes that we turn next.

8

A new hope

Star Wars is a movie about hope. In fact, in its special edition released in 1997, its subtitle was used more explicitly – *Star Wars: A New Hope*. Reflecting on his first sci-fi movie, *THX 1138*, which was very pessimistic and stressed how bad things were, Lucas said, 'I began to think that in order to do anything in film that will have social repercussions – you have to make an optimistic movie which gives hope. That way things can happen.'[76]

Mark Hamill, like the many fans who flocked to see it, was struck by the fact that *Star Wars* is 'very triumphant and very optimistic'. This theme was not just for *Star Wars: A New Hope*. Lucas was concerned that it informed the whole *Star Wars* project. During a script conference on *Return of the Jedi*, Lucas told Lawrence Kasdan, the writer, 'The whole emotion I am trying to get at the end of this film is for you to be emotionally and spiritually uplifted and to feel absolutely good about life. That is the greatest thing that we could ever possibly do.'[77]

Hope runs through *Star Wars*. Faced with the totalitarian

Empire wiping out the Rebellion, Princess Leia sends a message in R2-D2, which in the early stages of *Star Wars: A New Hope* is played six times: 'Help me Obi-Wan Kenobi, you're my only hope.' The whole story is based on the hope that the Rebels will restore freedom to the galaxy, that Luke, Leia and Han will survive and that all of this will work out well in the end, against impossible odds.

The two droids, C-3P0 and R2-D2, provide not just light relief or the basic narrative of the plot, but contrasting responses to the future. C-3P0 is the eternal pessimist, declaring that droids are 'made to suffer' and it's their 'lot in life'. In contrast, R2-D2 simply gets on with the mission of contacting Obi-Wan Kenobi, showing a great deal of faith in the final outcome.

Star Wars is not the only recent series of science-fiction movies to stress hope. Rick Berman, executive producer of *Star Trek: The Next Generation*, *Deep Space Nine* and *Voyager*, commenting at the twenty-fifth birthday celebration for the series, said, '*Star Trek* offers a future that is better than the present.' Kate Mulgrew, who plays Captain Kathryn Janeway, was more explicit when asked why *Star Trek* was so popular. 'It's basically about hope,' she replied.

Why is hope so important in *Star Wars*' popularity? A number of philosophers and theologians have recently become more interested in hope for the same reasons hope is so important in *Star Wars*: hope is fundamental to being human, but, at the turn of the millennium, Western societies are undergoing a crisis of hope.[78] Hope allows us to move out of those things which constrain us, but as we look back on the twentieth century where can we get hope from?

'Wars do not make one great'

Traditionally, hope came from belief in the 'myth of human progress'. Western culture was dominated by what philosophers call a 'metanarrative', an overarching story by which our society and its members lived. This great story or myth was that human history was basically a long march towards utopia, a state of perfection both for the society and the individual.

Indeed, some of the first works of science fiction were about the search for this perfection. Thomas More's *Utopia* (1516) and Francis Bacon's *New Atlantis* (1626) speculated on what such perfection would be. The path to utopia quickly became identified with the power of human beings to change the world. The Enlightenment gave confidence in human reason which, if purged from authority, prejudice and superstition, would lead to freedom and prosperity.

Such confidence seemed to be well placed. The power of human reason was shown in the success of science and technology. Put simply, if we could put men on the Moon then anything could be done. Around 1900 there was a great deal of optimism based on this confidence in human reason. Scientists believed that they had discovered just about everything that could be discovered, and universal education was widely reckoned to lead to a society of better moral values and less violence. Even Marxism believed in this myth of human progress. The mechanism, of course, was different from that of the capitalist world – constant class struggle and revolution would bring the progress.

The theories of biological evolution and natural selection

proposed by Charles Darwin also seemed to indicate that things were getting better. They gave a philosophical model of progress which was believed to apply to human societies. Just as living things had evolved to produce human reason, so human reason would push forward the evolution of society to rid the world of violence, disease and hunger.

In this myth of human progress, the power and responsibility for creating the future are human. There is no need for God, as human will and reason will sort everything out. This has been a major theme of the twentieth century and has been reflected in a great deal of science fiction. As Stephen May has pointed out, many science-fiction stories see hope as coming from technological progress.[79] In 1926, Hugo Gernsback founded the magazine *Amazing Stories*, which was illustrated with images of vast new cities and huge spaceships. In fact, Gernsback's own novel *Ralph 124C41+*, published in 1925, sees science and technology achieving utopia. Later in the century, Arthur C. Clarke was a great supporter of the idea that technology would lead to a better future. Even in *Independence Day* (1996) when faced by overwhelming odds and huge spaceships, the Earth is saved by (America's) human reason, missile power and computer viruses.

The trouble, however, is that the twentieth century does not give a lot of support to such confidence. The history of the last century exposes the myth of human progress as untrue and shatters its credibility. The optimism of 1900 was destroyed in the trenches of the First World War, when human reason and technology was not used to build a better world, but simply to slaughter more and more people. Such pessimism can be easily seen in cinema. *All Quiet on the Western Front* (1930) and *Saving Private Ryan* (1998) show the horrors of two world wars. *Schindler's List* (1993), *The Killing Fields* (1984) and *Cry Freedom* (1987) remind us of the holocaust and the mass murders of evil regimes. *The Deerhunter* (1978) and the movie that Lucas almost made, *Apocalypse Now* (1979), demonstrate that the US with all its technology and power makes monumental mistakes. *All the President's Men* (1976) shows the corruption of politicians who control the technology and power.

Wars, torture, famine and abuse of the environment do not make one great! Many people in Western societies may have been comforted by economic growth and affluent lifestyles, but the myth of human progress has not dealt with growing inequalities between rich and poor. This pessimism has also been reflected in science fiction. In the sixties, hope turned quickly to despair in books by authors such as J.G. Ballard. Science-fiction movies before *Star Wars* were not terribly optimistic or hopeful. Technological progress was seen to be out of control and ultimately threatening.

On the day that *Star Wars* opened in the UK, the BBC showed the first episode of Terry Nation's *Blake's Seven*, which ran for three years. This was also a story of rebels fighting an evil empire. In contrast they never won a victory and were ultimately defeated.

The theologian Jurgen Moltmann has pointed out that pride and despair contradict the true nature of hope.[80] In James Cameron's *Titanic* (1998) there is a graphic illustration of this. Pride in technology turns to despair at the sinking of the unsinkable.

'You're my only hope'

If the myth of human progress falls by the history of the twentieth century, where do we turn? Friedrich Nietzsche (1844–1900) saw the 'death of God', that is the lack of belief in God, as the end of truth and morality as objective and universal values. Without that, there was no meaning or progress in history.

His view was that history was merely cyclical. In *Groundhog Day* (1993), Bill Murray played a journalist stuck in a day which just repeated itself time after time and there was no way out. That was Nietzsche's view of history, an eternal recurrence of the same old events. If life is good you just enjoy it; if it is not there is no alternative. It is a view without hope.

Much can be said of the more modern alternative to the myth of progress, that is, postmodernism. This view argues that there is no overall story or narrative to be told. As one of its proponents, Jean-François Lyotard, says, the postmodern is characterised by 'incredulity towards metanarratives'. It has an emphasis on the present rather than the future and is again a view without hope.

When George Lucas was creating *Star Wars*, postmodernism had not fully developed, but he was writing in a time when there was a crisis of hope. As we have seen, the threat of nuclear war, the stalling of the space programme, Vietnam and the crisis in the economy meant that the myth of progress as a basis of hope was not working. The words above Dante's Hell, 'Abandon all hope, you who enter,' could easily be applied to Western society.

Such lack of hope leads to apathy. Luke, working on his

uncle's farm on Tatooine, is deprived of the hope of going to the academy. It leads to apathy in the present, and Obi-Wan Kenobi has to work very hard to get Luke to join the 'crusade'.

It seems that in *Star Wars*, Lucas was constructing an alternative metanarrative to the myth of progress or to the scepticism that would become postmodernism. To do this he not only used fantasy, but also relied on a much older meta-narrative.

Fantasy and hope

It is sometimes difficult to characterise *Star Wars* as science fiction or science fantasy. One definition of fantasy is, 'A fantasy is a story based on and controlled by an overt violation of what is generally accepted as possibility; it is the narrative result of transforming the condition contrary to fact into "fact" itself.'[81] This definition is helpful when applied to *Star Wars* in pointing out how hope is explored. Based in the 'real world' of identifiable humans and characters 'like us' in which hope is difficult to find, it encourages the imagination to believe that there is real hope and that good will win. The dominant pessimism is violated in a story of optimism.

Chris Kalabokes, the financial analyst at Fox in 1975, in his recommendation to the Fox board for the go-ahead on *Star Wars*, said, 'Good won out, and in the end, everyone was saved who had to be saved, and everyone bad was dealt with.'[82] This sense of 'closure' is both reassuring and satisfying.

Many have pointed out that it is the artists and poets of society who cling on to hope, especially in times of crisis or pessimism. Lucas uses a story to do this. The importance of this should not be underestimated. Frank Kermode has suggested that we deal with the chaos of the world by telling stories, and the end of the story is important as it gives meaning to the rest.[83] That Lucas chooses to end *Star Wars* with the good guys winning is a very simple statement of hope.

What, however, is this hope based on? *Star Wars* agrees that human power and technology by themselves do not give hope. The myth of human progress is symbolised by the Empire's Death Star, and indeed the part of the trilogy which ends without hope, in terms of the carbon freezing of Han Solo, is titled *The Empire Strikes Back*. Hope within *Star Wars* comes from the belief that there is something outside the normal processes of human will and reason, which is working for the good: the Force. Philosophers would call this 'belief in transcendence'.

When I gave a newspaper interview around the time of the US launch of *The Phantom Menace*, the reporter asked me what theology was in *Star Wars*. I replied that the concept of hope was one of the theological themes. The reporter pushed further, asking why hope was a theological theme? He was quite right to push further. After all, people hope in different ways. *Star Wars* is not the only movie about hope and optimism. The best is probably Capra's *It's a Wonderful Life* (1946) and the worst is dear Annie singing, 'the Sun'll come out tomorrow' (*Annie*, 1982). But Lucas bases his hope on the belief in transcendence. This is why hope is a theological theme.

The 'older metanarrative', which was prior to the myth of

human progress and remains an alternative to post-modernism, is the belief in God. Within the Western culture in which Lucas was writing, this was belief in the God of Christianity. Indeed, we can get some further insight into hope by looking at this Christian metanarrative.

The force of transcendence

This belief in transcendence has been the foundation of Christianity's belief in hope. Hope is not based on the belief that the world is getting better and better. Hope is grounded on a God who is beyond this universe and who comes to give us hope.

George Steiner has pointed out that the most creative people in art and poetry make a wager on the world and history having meaning and hope.[84] He calls it a wager on the meaningfulness of meaning.

The Christian makes a similar wager, but this wager is on the God of the resurrection. The resurrection disrupts this world's belief that death is the end and there is no hope, and offers the evidence that God will make things good in the end. Confidence is not placed in human beings or technology but in God.

In fact, many of the images about the future used in the New Testament focus on this. The New Testament says that in the future the world will encounter an 'Antichrist', a figure who symbolises evil and lies. This image is a reminder that the future is not simply progress to a better world. The 'parousia' is an image which says that sometime in the future Jesus

Christ will return in worldwide glory to bring in a new creation and a judgment of evil. These images speak of something God will do. Other images of the future speak of goodness, healing, celebration and the centrality of God and the fulfilment of the kingdom of God, such as creation as a garden city, future life being like sabbath rest or a marriage feast. These images are not meant to be understood primarily in a literal sense. Some groups take delight in identifying the Antichrist as everyone from Saddam Hussein to Bill Gates.

They are images which remind us that the myth of human progress is not the future, and that God's intervention in the future will end the story with the triumph of the good. The confidence of the Christian comes from faith not in the future, but in the God of the future. As Bauckham and Hart write, 'In faith we shall see duly, our imagination is engaged, stretched and enabled to accommodate a vision of a meaningful and hopeful future for the world, a meaning which could never be had by extrapolating the circumstances of the tragic drama of history itself.'[85]

Hope beyond death?

Christian hope is often characterised simply as the hope of immortality. At the end of *Return of the Jedi*, Obi-Wan Kenobi and Yoda are joined by the redeemed Anakin Skywalker in some kind of eternal spirit existence. This belief in continued existence after death is part of the belief of hope. Indeed, as the philosopher Stephen Clark has pointed out, it is one of the central themes of science fiction and fantasy. From the angelic elves of Tolkien's *The Lord of the Rings* to the pursuit of the eternal nexus in *Star Trek Generations* (1994), there is a desire to be liberated from death. Science fiction dreams of cryogenic freezing, uploading our information patterns onto computers and the rejuvenating properties of potions or other worlds such as in *Star Trek Insurrection* (1999).

Christian hope does promise that the individual goes beyond this life to a new life after death. But it is not only about that. It is also the hope of transformation and goodness now. When Karl Marx criticised religion as the opiate of the people, he was pointing out that some religion can become so otherworldly that it is of no earthly use.

However, Christian hope will not allow that. Jurgen Moltmann wrote, 'Those who hope in Christ can no longer put up with reality as it is.'[86] The Christian belief in a God of justice, love and goodness gives imagination and confidence to change things. Imagination allows us to transcend the limits of the present, whether it be our history, events or dominant ideas. We can envision how things might be different and be confident that they can be different. That trust and confidence is not in ourselves, or history, or technology, but in God. God is the guarantee that the future can be different, and in a world where so often evil seems to triumph we can believe that good will eventually triumph.

Hope in this sense reforms our view of the present. Luke, when given hope by the Force, takes on the responsibility to make a difference. The model is very similar to the Christian model. To believe that only God can supply a good conclusion to real life means that we work with him to achieve that. As Bauckham and Hart write, 'This means that those who live by this story live within it. It gives us our identity, our place in the story, and a part to play in the still-to-be-completed purposes of God for his world. Indeed the story is told precisely so that people may live by it.'[87]

Lucas in *Star Wars* is giving hope that all things will be good in the end. His story of a past civilisation in a galaxy far away, but in many ways like our own, sees hope located in the transcendent, that is, the Force working through the response of people. It is a story which offers hope without minimising evil.

Bruno Bettelheim, in speaking about the power of movies, suggests that the attraction of Yoda is as the reincarnation of the teddy bear of infancy we turn to for solace. He writes, 'Any vision of the future is really based on visions of the past, because that is all we can know for certain.'[88] Lucas is partly doing that, saying, Here is a story set in the past that turned out well, therefore there is hope for the future. But it is not only that. The transcendence of the story is here today in belief in God, thus the future can be welcomed and enjoyed. On a very personal level, that is where my Christian faith and my excitement with *Star Wars* interacted. *Star Wars* was giving confidence to the imagination to believe that things could change, and pointing towards the transcendent as a guarantee of that change. My Christian faith was filling out the nature of that transcendence in knowing God.

This undergirds the positive optimism of Lucas. In an interview in 1987 he said,

> The fact is that you can't hang on to the past. The
> future may be completely strange and scary, but that's

the way it should be. I thought that was one of the biggest challenges facing teenagers. I got to do what I wanted to do by not being frightened by the future and the unknown, and I figured that was a good message to get across... The idea is not to be afraid of change... *Star Wars* shows progression. You may be frightened – and it's sad because you are leaving something behind – but go forward. That's what life is about. You can either have a good attitude about change or a bad attitude about it. You can't fight tidal waves, you can only ride them. So the best thing to do is get your surfboard and make the best of it.[89]

Hope leads on to personal responsibility and motivation, and to that we turn next.

9

'Aren't you a little short for a stormtrooper?'

They were in the wrong place at the wrong time. Naturally they became heroes. Leia Organa of Alderaan, Senator.' So Lucas ends the prologue to his first *Star Wars* book.[90] This is a story about heroes and that is part of its appeal.

Joseph Campbell's book, *The Hero with a Thousand Faces*, came out in 1949. In it he argues that underneath the myths of folklore and religion there is a common archetype, that of the hero. As we have seen, Campbell had a huge influence on the thinking of Lucas, and also influenced others, including James Cameron, director of the *Terminator* movies.

Campbell goes further than just saying a hero is a constituent part of all mythological stories. He actually suggests that a 'hero's journey' is fundamental to the myth. This journey has a sequence to it. The hero is separated from the ordinary world, then undergoes trials or initiations, and then returns to share what he or she has achieved.

Campbell argues that this pattern is seen in such stories as

Jason, who leaves the Cave to search for the Golden Fleece, the Knights of the Round Table who seek the Holy Grail, and in the figures of every major religion. Thus, according to Campbell, Moses journeyed to Mount Sinai, moving from the everyday world to a place of supernatural wonder. There he received the Law and then returned to the people of Israel to share with them that Law. He suggests that the same pattern is seen in the story of Buddha and indeed in Jesus. For example, Campbell suggests that Jesus' forty days of temptation by Satan in the desert was his separation and sequence of trials.

Whether this pattern fits as well as Campbell thinks it does is uncertain. However, the pattern is there in broad outline in *Star Wars*. Luke Skywalker is a traditional adolescent hero who undergoes mythological rites of passage and accepts a mission against superhuman and supernatural odds.

'You must follow your own path; no one can choose it for you'

The first of Campbell's stages in the journey of the hero is the separation from common life and the call to adventure. This can be the result of an inner feeling or outside circumstances. It is often a supernatural call, helped by some wizard or spiritual mentor who gives advice and guidance. For Luke Skywalker all these things are involved. He is frustrated by the sense that his destiny lies beyond working on his uncle's farm. The arrival of the droids with the message from Princess Leia changes his life: the farm is destroyed and Obi-Wan Kenobi becomes his spiritual guide.

Obi-Wan has been characterised either as the wizard Merlin or a holy hermit. Certainly his desert lifestyle and his monk-like robes have echoes of religious teachers such as John the Baptist. He embodies wisdom in old age with a deep spirituality, becoming Luke's teacher in the ways of the Force. He also acts as a substitute father figure, which plays on the mystery surrounding Luke's father. He provides Luke with the goal of becoming a Jedi Knight and gives him a 'talisman', a lightsabre that belonged to Luke's father. There are echoes here of King Arthur and the sword Excalibur. Luke initially refuses the call to adventure, which again is characteristic of the hero's journey.

The call to adventure leads to an initial triumph, that of the success of the Rebel attack on the Death Star. Here Luke is aided by the continuing presence of Obi-Wan Kenobi in some kind of spirit existence. The firing of the proton torpedo into the thermal exhaust port has been likened to a hero slaying a dragon or to the biblical story of David taking on the giant Goliath and defeating him.

The second stage of the hero's journey is probably seen to fullest effect in *The Empire Strikes Back*. This is the stage of trials and initiation. Luke, through his response to the call to adventure, is now part of the Rebel mission. However he has much to learn, not least about the Force. He has to spend time with the Jedi Master Yoda and learns about failure. He faces evil within himself and is defeated, for the moment, by Vader.

The third stage of Campbell's journey is often identified with *Return of the Jedi*. Here Luke 'returns', transforming his new-found knowledge and skills into action. First he rescues Han Solo on his home planet of Tatooine and then faces a resurgence of evil represented by the new Death Star. Much has been read into this. Some have suggested that the Moon of Endor is an 'enchanted forest' with the furry Ewoks acting like helpful fairies! Some see Luke going with Vader into the second Death Star as the hero's 'descent into the underworld'. Certainly at this stage Luke is tested to the limit and has to face evil both inside and outside.

Whether Campbell's scheme can do justice to the complexity of world mythology, or whether Lucas's story actually fits with the scheme could be debated for some time. It has to be said that Campbell's view of the Christian story is, at the very least, eccentric. For example, he makes a very odd interpretation of the death and resurrection of Jesus in order to reconcile it with his hero's journey.[91]

However, what Campbell points to, and Lucas uses, is the powerful image of the hero. Why is this such a powerful theme?

'In your pursuit of peace and justice, remember, the Force will be with you... always'

What is it that grabs us about a hero? Part of it is the triumph of an individual over a system. *Star Wars* is about a hero who accomplishes his task of battling against an oppressive system. The Empire represents a totalitarian regime where individuality is opposed. Troops all wear the same uniforms and the faces of stormtroopers are never seen. When Vader attempts to tempt Luke to the dark side he says, 'with our combined strength we can end this destructive conflict and bring order to the galaxy'. But this order is the suppression of the individual by the system.

Joseph Campbell comments, 'Vader... is a bureaucrat living not in terms of himself but in terms of an imposed system. This is the threat to our lives that we all face today... How do you relate to the system so that you are not compulsively serving it?... By holding to your own ideals for yourself and, like Luke Skywalker, rejecting the system's impersonal claims upon you.'[92]

The power of the individual may be a very Western concept, reinforced by a market economy in which Margaret Thatcher once famously proclaimed, 'There is no community.' Indeed, spirituality in the West has become more and more centred on the individual. New Age beliefs focus on individual spiritual experience. In addition, what sociologists call the 'privatisation of belief' means that one person can believe one thing and another person believe another and, as long as the belief is internalised or kept private, different beliefs can be tolerated.

Star Wars may be attractive because it promotes individuality in the face of a conforming system. But the hero motif is more than that. The hero through individual courage accomplishes something for others. Thus Martin Luther King is seen as a hero, not just because of his refusal to conform to the expectations and stereotypes of racial injustice, but because in a very real way he led people towards the 'promised land'. Jesus of Nazareth in this sense was Martin Luther King's hero and is not dissimilar to the hero represented by Luke Skywalker. When Bob Dylan spoke of Jesus Christ as his hero at a concert in 1985, he was referring to the way Jesus stood up against a corrupt religious system and gave his own life for others. We admire courage, but it has to achieve something.

'When judging people size matters not'

Another part of the attraction of the hero motif in *Star Wars*, and many other stories, is that it can be true of an ordinary person. Teenagers identify with Luke Skywalker, and children identify with Anakin Skywalker, because here are ordinary people – at one level – who become heroes.

It is interesting that *Star Wars* offers one of the first strong female heroes in the person of Princess Leia. The seventies were a time of change for many women. The development of the women's movement, their right to choose on abortion, and new employment opportunities were changing the traditional stereotypes of women. By 1975, 50 per cent of US women held jobs outside the home. *Star Wars* reflects some tension about this. Aunt Beru seems to stay at home doing the cooking and making use of an early form of tupperware. In contrast Leia comes onto the screen firing her blaster, and demonstrates courage, ability and leadership. Sometimes she fulfils the role of hero, as when she takes over from Han and Luke and gets them all out of the prison block on the Death Star, while at other times she seems to have slipped back into the stereotype of the love interest who stands wringing her hands while the men go out to do battle.

Nevertheless, Leia is part of the development of the heroic woman in Hollywood movies. This would be seen supremely in

Sigourney Weaver's Ripley in the *Alien* movies. Indeed the last few years of the nineties have seen many more female heroic figures, no longer just in science-fiction movies. In 'slasher' movies such as *Scream* (1996) and *I Know What You Did Last Summer* (1997) the female, although initially seen as the victim, emerges as the hero who helps the men to defeat evil.

Star Wars shows that ordinary people, male and female, can become heroes. It is fair to say that this is limited by the fact that it is young, beautiful people in *Star Wars* who win the victory, but not entirely. Obi-Wan Kenobi is not young and Yoda cannot be described as beautiful!

Some years ago, the science-fiction writer and academic C.S. Lewis pointed out that science fiction tends to relegate character below plot. This is partly done because the setting is strange, and if the situation is strange then to have peculiar people as well would be an 'oddity too much'.[93]

The main heroes in *Star Wars* are immediately identifiable. Although in a galaxy far, far away, they are identifiable as human beings, with the same kinds of emotions and problems. Luke's dysfunctional family, his teenage rebellion and inner emotions build a bridge to the audience. That bridge allows the story to develop in a way which raises the question for the individual of 'Can I be a hero like that?' It may not be defeating Darth Vader but it may be about resisting an oppressive system whether racism, sexism or another injustice.

As Lucas comments in an interview in *Time* magazine, 'Heroes come in all sizes, and you don't have to be a giant hero. You can be a very small hero. It's just as important to understand that accepting self-responsibility for the things you do, having good manners, caring about other people – these are heroic acts. Everyone has the choice of being a hero every day of their lives. You don't have to get into a giant laser-sword fight and blow up three spaceships to become a hero.'[94]

How to become a hero

Thus the story of the hero becomes the motivation for personal responsibility. Lucas wanted his story to encourage individual responsibility and moral character. The hero cannot run away from his or her fate. Responsibility cannot be avoided.

Rick McCallum, producer of The Phantom Menace, comments, 'The story is meaningful simply because there's an age of longing that people go through. That's what the story is about – longing, yearning. We ask ourselves, What's next? Can I be the person I want to be? For some the dream comes true. For some it doesn't. We look at the story of Anakin Skywalker, and it makes us wonder, Is that just a cast of the die? Is it our character? Is it luck?'[95]

Once again Lucas's own background is important in this. Orville Schell sums this up when he writes, 'By sidestepping the monolithic Hollywood studio system – which one might interpret as being an animating force behind his notion of the "Empire" – and by creating his own alternative movieland structure, he is living proof that a "little guy" with an alternative vision, who grew up the son of a stationery-store owner in Modesto, California, can still prevail in America.'[96]

Lucas has fashioned a story about heroes who take responsibility by individual action, becoming involved in a bigger quest. Indeed, we only find ourselves by responding to such a call. Selfishness makes us subhuman. Such heroes of selflessness give us models to follow. Lucas comments, 'The story in *Star Wars* is about heroes who have the ideals that we as a society would like people to possess. There's a certain part of society that would like everyone to be cynical. But at the same time, another segment needs to have heroes – to have somebody of whom they can say: "This is the kind of person we should aspire to be."'[97]

In the light of Watergate and Vietnam, the US was looking for heroes. We still are today. Jack Sorenson, President of LucasArts, said, 'I believe that *Star Wars* is the mythology of a non-sectarian world. It describes how people want to live. People all view politics as corrupt, and yet people are not so cynical underneath; they want to believe in something pure, something noble. That's *Star Wars*.'[98]

Yet the motif of heroes in *Star Wars* goes beyond this. Some see in heroes a kind of escapism. It is easier to spectate as Superman or Batman triumph over evil, than fight against such evils as racism or world debt in our everyday life. That is certainly true for many, but heroes also inspire us with what is possible. Lawrence Kasdan, the screenwriter on *The Empire Strikes Back* and *Return of the Jedi*, said about *Star Wars*, 'After you saw it, you thought, "My God, anything is possible."'[99]

The myth is about hope. Without hope there is no reason to be a hero. If nothing matters, if things cannot be different, if we don't know that things will turn out alright in the end then there is no point in doing anything. Hope makes heroes. As we have seen, the hope in *Star Wars* is based on a belief in transcendence. The hero is only able to triumph through supernatural help. Luke only slays the Goliath of the Death

Star by trusting in the unseen Force. If you want to be a hero, then you need that kind of help.

Is Luke Skywalker Jesus?

Luke Skywalker was voted a more popular role model than Jesus in a recent American poll. Some religious groups condemned American society for such a belief, while others claimed that Luke Skywalker was in fact based on Jesus.

Whatever one believes about this, I am drawn in the analysis of the hero's journey to a strong parallel to the Christian faith. The story of Luke Skywalker works in some similar ways to the story of Jesus. As a teenager I found myself inspired by Luke, Leia and Han. Of course, much of that was emotional escapism. Nevertheless, my imagination was stretched and challenged by the hero story.

Perhaps I connected with it so much because, at the same time, my imagination was being stretched and challenged by the story of Jesus. The hero's journey of Jesus is a call from his Father to live as a common carpenter and then to stand for justice for the oppressed and bring freedom to those in bondage. The journey ends in his death on the cross for all the world. The resurrection gives hope that this kind of hero's journey is the way to go, and I was challenged to follow it. The only way that I could follow was if God gave me the help to do it. The story of Jesus is about belief in transcendence, which meant a change to my lifestyle and moral values.

Whether that is simply emotional escapism is a question we will need to return to.

10

'The boy is dangerous...'

How can Anakin Skywalker turn into Darth Vader? This is the subject of Episodes II and III of the *Star Wars* saga, but the question runs through all of the movies. Why is Darth Vader so evil? Will Luke be seduced by the dark side? How can evil be defeated?

Good and evil are fundamental to the story of *Star Wars*. The journalist, Darren Bignell, sees the story of the hero as, 'the whole caboodle cloaked in a near-biblical theme of some small vestige of good rebelling against the indomitable tyranny of evil'.[100] In fact the struggle of good and evil in *Star Wars* is nearer to the biblical theme than some people think.

All-encompassing darkness?

It seems to me that sometimes writers on *Star Wars* get a little carried away. For example, Mary Henderson describes the central characters in terms of 'Vader as the all-encompassing darkness out of which Luke shines as the sun and Leia as the moon'.[101] That may be taking the mythology too far, but it has to be acknowledged that there is a clear distinction between good and evil, with Darth Vader appearing originally as the embodiment of evil.

When Darth Vader first appears in *Star Wars*, he arrives in a passageway following an explosion, and everyone instinctively backs away. His first encounter with Leia is a stark contrast of his black robes and face mask with her white robe embodying the forces of good. Some have suggested that Vader represents the Jungian archetype of evil with mask, black armour and robes. He is the personification of evil working to destroy the good.

In *The Phantom Menace*, evil is even more graphic. Darth Maul is an icon of evil and fear. The image is not unlike Satan, complete with aggressive red colouring and horns. Through these characters, and indeed the characters of the Emperor and Darth Sidious, Lucas is very simply stating that evil is real, it is a major force in the universe, and it needs to be opposed.

It has been argued that this clear distinction between good and evil has its roots in Zoroastrian belief. This religion, dating back to the sixth or seventh century BC in Persia, saw two fundamentally opposing forces in the universe, arising from the good creator, Ahura Mazda, and the evil spirit, Angra Mainyu, whose purpose was to destroy and harm creation.

At a surface level there does seem to be a clear distinction between good and evil in *Star Wars*. Indeed, evil needs to be wiped out. For example, the Death Star is totally obliterated. No one tries to save the stormtroopers, who no doubt were being manipulated by the evil system.

However, Lucas's understanding of good and evil is much

more complex and indeed subtle. Such an understanding is based more on Christianity than it is on Zoroastrianism. In Zoroastrian belief, evil is outside the human individual who is naturally good. Both *Star Wars* and Christianity see the individual as a little more complex.

'Anger, fear and aggression lead to the dark side'

Evil is not just to be fought as an outside force, it is also to be fought within. As the *Star Wars* saga develops, Lucas is careful to develop themes of evil and temptation in terms of 'the power of the dark side'.

Vader may be represented as the legendary monster but the dark side can affect all of us. Already in *Star Wars: A New Hope*, evil at the level of the human spirit is touched on. Luke's Aunt Beru says to Uncle Owen that there is 'too much of his father in him'. The primary reference is to Luke's sense of adventure and impetuosity but, as we see later, such things when uncontrolled lead to the dark side. Obi-Wan Kenobi referring to Luke's father calls him a 'good friend' and then goes on to say that Darth Vader 'betrayed and murdered your father'. Anakin Skywalker was 'seduced by the dark side' and Luke may experience the same thing.

In *The Empire Strikes Back* this conflict at the level of the human spirit is developed, alongside the conflict at the level of the universe. Yoda sends Luke into the mystic tree cave which is 'strong with the dark side of the Force'. What Luke experiences is his own dark side: impatience, violence and hostility. Encountering Vader in the cave he fights a battle and eventually kills Vader, but then sees his own face within Vader's helmet. He realises that Darth Vader is not simply some external evil presence but the shadow side of Luke himself. The dark side of the Force lies within as well as without.

As Luke struggles with the dark side, so Vader seems to be struggling with his good side. Vader's refusal to kill Luke shows he still has some small measure of good within. Mary Henderson helpfully comments, 'One personifies evil but carries within him the potential for redemption, while the other personifies good but carries within the potential for evil. Beyond the struggle between them lies the hope of their reconciliation through atonement.'[102] To this reconciliation and atonement we will need to return in the next chapter, but it is enough to notice at present that the division between good and evil at the level of the human spirit is not absolute.

Lucas plays on this throughout the saga. The final scene of *The Empire Strikes Back* shows Luke with a mechanical arm. As Vader is half human and half machine the symbolism is clear. Might Luke become like Vader? *The Phantom Menace* represents this theme also. Although Darth Maul may be the representation of evil and fear, he is not detached completely. In contrasting his chief villain with Vader who is half machine, Lucas says, 'This one is all human. I wanted him to be an alien, but I wanted him to be human enough that we could identify with him... he's the evil within us.'[103]

Where does the evil within us come from, and why does it have power over us? What evil lies within Senator Palpatine

111

that will eventually manifest itself fully as the evil Emperor? Why will Anakin turn to the dark side? These are fundamental questions for Lucas. 'What is it in the human brain that gives us the capacity to be as evil as human beings have been in the past and are right now?' he asks. 'I think it comes out of a rationale of doing certain things and denying to yourself that you're actually doing them.'[104] Commenting on what will turn Anakin to the dark side he says, 'The issue of greed, of getting things and owning things and having things, is the opposite of compassion – of not thinking of yourself all of the time.'[105]

Evil arises from bad choices, but those choices are affected by the tempting presence of evil outside of us – whether you locate that in a system, other individuals or in a personal spiritual evil that Christians have traditionally called Satan. Joseph Campbell points out, '*Star Wars* is not a simple morality play, it has to do with powers of life as they are either fulfilled or broken and suppressed through the action of men.'[106]

So good and evil are given a complex relationship. Where does that come from?

Falling for the dark side

Mary Henderson points towards Christianity as providing the basis of this understanding of evil and the theme of redemption which we will look at in the next chapter. However, she then gives a rather confused summary of the Christian understanding:

According to St Augustine, Adam and Eve are created of the goodness of God, but when they are successfully tempted by Satan to eat of the tree of good and evil, they are born again in the devil.[107]

It is important to clarify this, and we will see that Henderson is right in pointing to Christianity, but confused in her understanding of Christianity. In fact, properly understood, the doctrine of evil in Christianity seems to provide the basis, whether knowingly or unknowingly, to the concept Lucas uses in *Star Wars*.

Why is the nature of human beings so complex in their relationship with good and evil? The Christian faith believes in the goodness of men and women as created by a good God. Made in his image, we reflect creativity, love, compassion and the desire for justice that are characteristic of God himself. But, if that is the case, why do we do evil to one another and to the environment? The Bible answers that, not by advancing a philosophical theory as to the origin of evil, but by telling a story.

It is a story of how Adam and Eve fell from the perfect relationship they had with God. The Adam and Eve story has often been neglected because of the debate about whether it can be reconciled with modern science. I have written about this elsewhere, but it is a shame if such a debate means that we do not hear the truth of the story.[108]

Adam and Eve represent people as God wanted them to be. He gave them responsibility to look after the world, the capacity for intimate relationship with himself and the freedom to make their own choices. They were not to be 'battle droids', to simply do the will of a tyrant, or a 'Truman' figure whose freedom is only an illusion.

Adam and Eve listened to the suggestion of the serpent and disobeyed God. The result of that disobedience was that their relationship with God was broken. This in turn affected their ability to use responsibility wisely to look after the world and limited their freedom to make choices. That is, this 'fall' led to a bias towards sin, which is our inner tendency to go our own way rather than God's way. Human beings are therefore a complex mixture of good and a bias towards sin.

The story of Adam and Eve is not just about how it all began, it is also a picture of how evil works in each human being. Lawrence Kasdan, commenting on the conflict between good and evil illustrated in *Star Wars*, simply says, 'life works out that way'.[109] There does seem to be a conflict within us about which way to go and a lure or temptation to the 'dark side'.

We set ourselves standards to live by, but are unable to live up to those standards. Our selfishness taints all of our lives. Mary Henderson's quote about Augustine, a Christian theologian of the fourth century, is misleading. Rather than being born again in the devil, Augustine viewed this inability to do the good thing as perverted self-love which affects each one of us. John Calvin, in the sixteenth century, built on this by saying that such selfishness arises out of disobedience against God.

Thus, the Christian picture recognises, as *Star Wars* does, the battle between good and evil within us. Vader is seduced by the dark side in order to control others and indeed the galaxy. Senator Palpatine is tempted also, his good motives being tainted by selfishness and greed for power.

Battling against the dark side

Yet Christianity also recognises, once again with *Star Wars*, the existence of evil outside the human spirit. Luke Skywalker does not simply battle with his own inner feelings. Vader, and the even more powerful Emperor, tempt Luke to choose the dark side. Luke has to battle with those influences, which attempt to exploit his own inner feelings.

In the Adam and Eve story, it is the serpent who encourages them to disobey God. Within the Bible, the serpent represents Satan, the leader of the spiritual forces who are at war with God. He personifies all that is evil and opposed to God, rebelling against God because of his own pride. His purpose is to pervert God's work in the universe. He has power but is not as powerful as God.

Darth Maul is a Satan figure: he is evil through and through, and even has the red skin and horns so beloved of medieval representations of Satan. Christians today have different interpretations of Satan. Some see him as a real being, others see him as a metaphor to express the fact that not all evil comes from within.

Whatever the interpretation of Satan, or indeed of Darth Maul, *Star Wars* reflects the Christian view that the battle against evil works on two levels, both within and without the individual. Thus Christians are committed to changing evils in society *and* to the inner transformation of individuals. In answer to Lucas's question that underpins Episodes I to III – 'How does a good person turn bad?'[110] – Christianity gives the answer: selfishness within, and pressure from outside.

The question now arises, How can evil be defeated? In the

closing scenes of *The Empire Strikes Back*, Luke is confronted by Vader in Cloud City. As we have seen, rather than surrender to the dark side Luke chooses death, throwing himself off a gantry. As it happens, his fall is broken and he survives. Nevertheless, the symbol of self-sacrifice as a way to defeat evil is central to *Star Wars* and indeed is central again to Christianity. It is to this theme that we turn next.

11

'I will grow more powerful than you can possibly imagine…'

An old *Star Wars* joke is the one which says that when he was struck down by Darth Vader's lightsabre, Obi-Wan Kenobi became 'Obi-Two Kenobies'. Yet this is a defining moment in *Star Wars*, full of religious symbolism and indeed mystery. Sir Alec Guinness did not take kindly initially to dying halfway through the movie, yet this remains one of the classic moments of modern cinema.

The scene is played out on the Empire's Death Star. Obi-Wan Kenobi has disabled the tractor beam, giving the *Millennium Falcon* the chance to escape. Luke, Leia, Han, Chewbacca and the droids are attempting to reach the ship. Obi-Wan Kenobi, realising that he needs to distract the guards, faces and begins to duel with Darth Vader. He then consciously decides to let Vader strike him down, saying that if Vader does this, 'I will grow more powerful than you can possibly imagine.'

His death is somewhat mysterious, his body disappearing from within his cloak. Initially you wonder whether he is dead or not. Obi-Wan Kenobi's words are fulfilled: his death acts as a distraction to allow the Rebel band to escape with the plans of the Death Star, and he appears in a vision to Luke, guiding him to use the Force to destroy the Death Star. This vision of Obi-Wan Kenobi, also seen in *The Empire Strikes Back* and *Return of the Jedi*, has been interpreted as some kind of resurrection and ascension motif.

It is even more interesting when put alongside Campbell's mythological journey of the hero. In many myths and legends the hero slays the monster, but here the monster slays Obi-Wan Kenobi. This is more than just some descent into the experience of death – the life given freely ultimately achieves victory over evil.

As we have seen in *The Empire Strikes Back*, Luke symbolises another act of self-sacrifice, choosing death rather than joining Vader in using the dark side of the Force to rule the galaxy. But the greatest moment of self-sacrifice happens at the end of *Return of the Jedi*.

How do we get Anakin back?

In early script discussions of this final meeting between Luke and the Emperor a number of possibilities were considered. The meeting was going to happen in the Emperor's chambers and all the designs had religious aspects. One was that of an underground cave within which was a lake of lava – not too far away from hell! Another was within a city of pyramids, and yet another in a cathedral-like structure. It is clear from this that Lucas had an encounter in mind which was going to have religious significance. Finally, the interior of the Death Star was chosen, partly for practical reasons and partly to contrast its cold technological sterility with the lush green environment of Endor.

Confronted by Vader and the Emperor within the new Death Star, and with the Rebel fleet suffering great losses, Luke attacks Vader in anger. Luke defeats Vader in the lightsabre duel and the Emperor urges Luke to finish him off. Luke sees his own mechanical hand and realises that he is on the way to becoming the next Vader, following the same path to evil as his father.

It is at this point that Luke once again resists being seduced by the dark side. He casts aside his lightsabre, mastering his anger and refusing to obey the Emperor's command. The Emperor turns on Luke using his dark powers. Luke appeals to his father for help, and Vader, at the cost of his own life, intervenes to destroy the Emperor. Vader becomes hero and saviour through his own self-sacrifice.

As Vader is dying he asks Luke to remove his mask. Vader's face, though scarred, is yet 'unformed' and 'undifferentiated'.[111] Joseph Campbell makes the point that this shows that you cannot develop your humanity by serving a system. Perhaps he should have gone on to say that the process of becoming fully human involves giving your life for others, for Luke then sees Vader transformed back to Anakin Skywalker, joining Yoda and Obi-Wan Kenobi in a 'heavenly vision'.

The religious symbols and motifs in this ending of the *Star Wars* trilogy are numerous and heavily interpreted by many people. Some have suggested that this is primarily about the reconciliation of Luke with his father. Luke has to admit dependence on Vader, asking his father to help him. The rediscovery of the 'child within' is certainly involved but is not all that is going on here.

As always, other interpretations need to have some contact with George Lucas's own understanding. The question is, How do you defeat evil without becoming evil yourself? One option for Luke is to use strength and fury, but 'anger, fear and aggression lead to the dark side'. Lucas comments, 'And it's only in the last act – when he throws his sword down and says, "I'm not going to fight this" – that he makes a more conscious, rational decision. And he does it at the risk of his life, because the Emperor is going to kill him. It's only that way that he is able to redeem his father... How do we get Darth Vader back? How do we get him back to that little boy that he was in the first movie, that good person who loved and was generous and kind?'[112] Lucas answers his question with, 'Ultimately Vader is redeemed by his children and especially by having children.'[113] Some have further speculated on whether this expresses something about Lucas's own experience in finding fulfilment in his children.

However, at another level this is very religious language. Here we have concepts of sacrifice, redemption and salvation. Rick McCallum, the producer of *The Phantom Menace*, says that in the whole saga of *Star Wars* we see Darth Vader 'and the choices he makes. And then of course in *Jedi* we see his redemption.'[114]

When Qui-Gon Jinn meets the slave boy Anakin he wonders whether this is the boy who will fulfil the prophecy of bringing balance to the Force. As the story unfolds we know that this boy will grow up, train as a Jedi, and marry Queen Amidala. They have two children, Luke and Leia. However, Anakin is corrupted and becomes Darth Vader. In one sense the children do redeem Vader, but Vader is restored to Anakin through defeating the evil Emperor by self-sacrifice. Peace and justice are restored to the galaxy by the boy Anakin, but through a mysterious and complicated route and through his own death.

Mary Henderson once again makes links with Christianity, commenting that in *Return of the Jedi* the redemption of the father is reminiscent of Christianity.[115] She fails to develop the comment or justify it to any great extent. However, it can be justified through consideration of the 'saviour figure' and the concept of redemption.

The boy who would be saviour

The hero in Campbell's analysis of world mythology is a saviour. After undergoing trials, the hero comes back to share the benefits with all. Indeed this concept of a saviour figure is powerful within cinema.

It has a long history. In the early development of cinema, saviour figures were quite common. This was in large part due to the fact that the Bible was one of the first stories to be adapted for the screen, as it was both popular and dignified, and also allowed some sex and violence to be acceptable because of the 'religious' context.

Cecil B. De Mille's *The Ten Commandments* (1923) and *The*

King of Kings (1927) showed Moses and Jesus as heroes and saviours of others. In subsequent years the figure of Jesus held a particular fascination, whether it be in William Wyler's *Ben Hur* (1959) or Martin Scorsese's *The Last Temptation of Christ* (1988).

These, of course, were specifically religious films. However, these themes have been explored in many other films outside of the 'religious' movie genre. One critic comments, 'Perhaps the true successors to the classic cinematic portrayals of Moses are the big-budget sensations of modern science-fiction cinema.'[116]

The academic Gaye Ortiz goes even further. She writes, 'many film heroes are in fact Christ figures who experience the kinds of things Christ did or who personify the righteous, loving, self-sacrificing Christ'.[117] She illustrates her suggestion with reference to a number of films such as *Superman* (1978) and its sequels, Clint Eastwood in such movies as *The Good, the Bad and the Ugly* (1966) and even *E.T. The Extra-Terrestrial* (1982)! She continues, 'There is no way one can equate the life of Christ with the story of *E.T.*, but there are serious parallels in the story which are difficult to ignore: E.T... suffered a death and resurrection and ascended to his original home. More significantly, his was a message of unconditional love, much like that seen in the crucified Christ.'[118]

This is not too surprising. The figure of Jesus has been admired and adopted by different cultures, especially within Western culture. Historians agree that the West owes a great deal to the influence of Christianity in the development of science, art, law and politics. At the centre of Christianity stands Jesus as saviour and redeemer. Born to poor parents through a virgin birth, Jesus was to fulfil the prophecy given in the Old Testament concerning the Messiah, God's chosen one. The word 'redemption' is about the buying back of someone from slavery. It is about a price being paid which leads to freedom.

We have seen already how Anakin Skywalker is modelled on such a figure. However, there are some important divergences between the figure of Jesus and Anakin. Jesus, though tempted by Satan, does not sin. His concern is for the poor and marginalised, and he uses his spiritual power to bring healing to those in need. He teaches about God and invites people to repent, that is to forsake earthly obsessions and turn in trust to God. Anakin, in contrast, is seduced by the dark side, wanting power and control over the galaxy.

'There are alternatives to fighting'

The prophecies about Jesus talk of his role as saviour and redeemer, not in terms of power but in terms of suffering. The redeemer is the one who will who suffer and die on behalf of others. The price of redemption is self-sacrifice. So, for example, in the Old Testament book of Isaiah the prophet speaks of one who was 'pierced for our transgressions, he was crushed for our iniquities; the punishment that brought us peace was upon him, and by his wounds we are healed'.[119] Christians have seen that passage clearly fulfilled in the torture and death of Jesus. He was arrested, abused, and then crucified.

Here is a picture of God that can be compared with the one

we discussed earlier, that of Christof, the director of *The Truman Show*. Christof is heartless and detached, never entering Truman's world, simply viewing it from on high. It is a popular view of God, but not a Christian view. Christians believe that because of God's love for people he entered this world in Jesus and gave himself for human beings by dying on the cross, taking the punishment for sin in their place.

However, death was not the end. Jesus was raised from the grave to new life. This new life was not just a resuscitation of the old body, but a new existence. Jesus was the same, in that he was recognisable from the nail prints in his hands, but he was also transformed, seemingly able to appear in rooms where the doors were locked. Through his death and resurrection Christians believe that sin is both forgiven and conquered and a new start in life can happen. As a Christian I have to admit that I do not understand the answer to a number of questions about this, for example, Why did God choose this method to die at that particular time in human history? I do know that forgiving someone does involve cost to the person who forgives. I also know that this experience of forgiveness from God is real in my own life.

At this point the story of *Star Wars* begins to resonate again with the biblical account. Rather than one character fulfilling the 'Christ' figure, a number of these themes are picked up by different characters. Obi-Wan Kenobi gives his life for the freedom of others. His death is somewhat mysterious but is not the end. A form of resurrection seems to take place. Indeed, the same is true ultimately of Anakin Skywalker. His self-sacrifice saves Luke and himself and he too experiences some form of resurrection. He fulfils the prophecy, but the mechanism of how he does this is complex and mysterious.

Saviours transform people's lives and lead them to new life. In Obi-Wan Kenobi, in Luke and Leia, and eventually in Anakin Skywalker, we see elements of Jesus – the man Christians have always claimed is saviour of the world.

The *Star Wars* redemption

George Lucas is not the only film-maker to explore the theme of redemption, or to base his hero on the insights of Joseph Campbell. James Cameron used Campbell's hero figure in his movies *The Terminator* (1984) and *Terminator II: Judgment Day* (1991). These movies centre around the struggle of Sarah Connor and her son John to avoid being terminated by cyborgs from the future. In the future the world has been taken over by artificial life forms who were originally created to provide national security. They turn on their creators and attempt to snuff out a resistance movement by sending 'terminators' back through time to kill Sarah, and her son John, who will become the leader of the movement. The movies deal with questions of technology gone wrong, and human responsibility for creating that technology.

In *Terminator II*, the killing machine is a T-1000. An earlier-model Terminator is sent back by the resistance to protect Sarah and John. As this Terminator protects them, so he begins to experience what it means to be human. In the final scene he sacrifices himself in an act of self-destruction, to prevent the future developing into the nightmare from which he has come. This is a truly human and heroic act. As Jesus said and demonstrated, 'No one has greater love than this, to lay down one's life for one's friends.'[120]

It is a picture of redemption similar to the actions of Obi-Wan Kenobi and Anakin Skywalker. Redemption is about personal cost in saving others. *The Shawshank Redemption* (1995) also picks up this theme. Tim Robbins plays Andy Dufresne, who shows that in prison the human spirit cannot be quenched and one individual can make a difference to others.

Why is redemption such a strong theme? From Batman to E.T. we seem to need a saviour figure. A major part of the answer is that we realise that as human beings we need help. The astronomer Sir Fred Hoyle pointed out that this was the motivation for believing in extraterrestrial intelligence, 'the expectation that we are going to be saved from ourselves by some miraculous interstellar intervention'.[121]

We desire help and we often seek it from the 'hero-outsider', sometimes a supernatural being, sometimes a good human. In *Star Wars*, the characters are not supernatural; redemption is dependent not just on the characters, but on the power of the Force. We need some kind of outside help.

But we must *want* that redemption. Darth Vader, strongly influenced by the dark side of the Force, is redeemed because he wants to save his son. On the other hand, Darth Maul and the Emperor seem to be so utterly overtaken by evil that they do not want a way out.

Lucas is offering a model of redemption based on self-sacrifice and personal responsibility – again to a large extent based on the Christian tradition in which Jesus is the supreme example.

12

Feel the Force

Sir Alec Guinness tells that during a Roman Catholic Mass, a fellow worshipper turned to him and said, 'May the Force be with you.' Sir Alec almost automatically replied, 'And also with you,' and then felt rather silly.[122] Perhaps it has something to do with the character of Obi-Wan Kenobi which provokes such greetings. Ewan McGregor tells of similar experiences, but his reply is a rather more direct, 'Don't be ridiculous!'[123]

In the previous chapters we have seen that belief in the transcendent is central to the story of *Star Wars*. It is the basis of hope, the inspiration for the hero's journey and the supernatural help needed to defeat evil and achieve redemption. Lucas uses the Force to convey that sense of the transcendent. The fact that some have taken it too far means that we must carefully examine what Lucas does with the Force. Is it religion or is it ridiculous?

'It binds the galaxy together'

What is the Force? Lucas has expanded the concept of the Force from Carlos Castaneda's phrase 'life force'. However, he does not give a fully worked-out philosophy of the Force. Helpful as it would be to books like this, and indeed for those who want to make a religion out of it, such a philosophy lecture would not fit well with an action movie. The fragmentary glimpses from the dialogue into the nature of the Force do remind us that Lucas does not want to suggest that the Force is worthy of devotion, but that it acts as a pointer to deeper questions.

As Luke and Obi-Wan discuss the Force during Luke's initial training, Luke asks whether the Force controls your actions. Obi-Wan replies, 'partially, but it also obeys your commands... The Force is what gives the Jedi his power. It's an energy field created by all living things. It surrounds us and penetrates us. It binds the galaxy together.' At this point the sceptic Han Solo says he has no evidence for it and it is 'no match for a good blaster'. The irony is strong. Solo will on many occasions be saved by the power of the Force.

When Luke goes to the swamp planet of Dagobah, the Jedi Master Yoda speaks of the Force in images more reminiscent of Eastern philosophies such as Buddhism. The Force is to be used only for 'knowledge and defence'. It gives the ability to foresee certain events and to move external objects with the power of the mind alone. Knowledge of the Force comes from training under a master and by means of direct intuitive insights, and should lead to calmness and peace.

The Force also has a dark side which leads to evil. When embracing the dark side it seems to be a downward spiral taking you deeper into evil. Both Vader and the Emperor use the power of the Force for such evil.

The Force itself can be used for good or evil, but can affect choices. Relating to it or using it depends more on the feelings rather than the mind, so that Obi-Wan Kenobi urges Luke, 'Use the Force... Let go.'

Attempted definitions abound. One definition puts it as 'a sort of spiritual substrate to the universe, into which human beings can plug themselves in order to perform amazing mental feats – or, to be honest, magic.'[124] Scott Athorne suggests that it is 'a natural energy field that suffuses the galaxy. It is generated by living things, and can be manipulated.'[125] However, the *Star Wars Encyclopedia* sees it as more than just an energy field, calling it 'both a natural and mystical presence'.[126]

In *The Phantom Menace* we learn a little more of the nature of the Force. The Jedi Knights were founded as a theological and philosophical study group and had become aware of the presence of the Force only gradually. Studying the Force they began to see that, in order to master its power, they needed to give 'service to the greater community and implementation of a system of laws that would guarantee equal justice for all'.[127] Thus the Jedi had become peacemakers throughout the galaxy.

Anakin Skywalker has a very high midi-chlorian count in his blood. Qui-Jon believes that he was conceived by midi-chlorians rather than by human contact. The midi-chlorians are described as the 'connectors to the Force itself'. They are microscopic life forms that reside within the cells of all living things and communicate with the Force. They are symbionts – life forms living together for mutual advantage. It is the midi-chlorians that speak to the Jedi, telling them 'the will of the Force'.[128]

It is an interesting construction, refined over three decades by Lucas. Yet it is not meant to be a comprehensive philosophy of life. The Force is complex, having elements of passive Oriental philosophies and the Judeo-Christian ethic of responsibility and self-sacrifice. It is not meant to be God, but to embody faith in a spiritual power. It is meant to point us to the transcendent, and say that there is more to the universe than just scientific materialism.

Lucas comments, 'The Force is what happens in spite of us, that we can either use or not use. We can fight these changes, or we can use them, incorporate them into our lives, take full advantage of them.'[129] It is not the Force itself that is important, it is what it points us to.

'No match for a good blaster'

Why is the Force so essential to Star Wars, and why has it captured people's imagination? Within the story it acts to make a contrast between transcendence and technology.

The Star Wars saga is full of technology, whether the use of special effects or in the spaceships, blasters or droids. Some have seen this as the major part of Star Wars, suggesting that Lucas is trying to give us a vision of our own future. The space programme did instil in Lucas the belief of a future in space, but the technology is not meant to be an end in itself.

Indeed, any discussion about the 'science' of Star Wars may sell a few books but is in the end pointless. It is reminiscent of the famous dispute between Jules Verne and H.G. Wells on how to get to the Moon. Verne thought Wells' antigravity substance was silly and Wells pointed out that Verne's giant propulsion gun would turn its human contents into 'strawberry jam'.[130]

Those who have studied the scientific questions involved come to somewhat boring conclusions. As C.J. Cherryh writes, in reality 'the most wonderful thrilling battle in space... demands more calculations than a Rubik's cube and is about as exciting as watching your dog scratch flees'.[131] But that does not matter to *Star Wars*. Robert Watts, co-producer of *Return of the Jedi*, says, '*Star Wars* has the freedom to say anything can happen in those days. Therefore you don't have to explain that landspeeders or sail barges work on anti-gravitational systems. There's no relationship to Earth.'[132]

Lucas reinforces the point: 'It's very surreal and bizarre and has nothing to do with science. I wanted it to be an adventure in space, like *John Carter on Mars*. That was before science took over, and everything got very serious and science-orientated. *Star Wars* has more to do with disclaiming science than anything else... It's a totally different galaxy with a totally different way of thinking. It's not based on science, which bogs you down. I don't want the movie to be about anything that would happen or be real. I wanted to tell a fantasy story.'[133]

The question then is, Why is there so much technology? Although this is a fantasy story, Lucas works hard to give the story some continuity with human existence on the Earth. The technology is not totally surreal and the artwork is based on images from all over the world. This is to give the audience some connection and familiarity with the *Star Wars* universe, but also to illustrate a central theological point: the tension between technology and the individual spirit. It is the story of the battle between the growth of technology and individual human spirituality or, as Lucas puts it, 'the idea of rocket ships and lasers up against somebody with a stick'.[134]

Faith in an ancient religion?

As we have already seen, this conflict between humanity and machine surfaces on a number of levels. Lucas created *Star Wars* against a background where technology was both idealised and demonised. Vietnam could not be won by technology, yet men were able to walk on the Moon. The beginnings of the environmental movement and the threat of the nuclear destruction of the planet went hand-in-hand with technological progress in a consumer society.

In *THX 1138* Lucas envisioned a soulless society with humans as simply cogs in the machine. In *Star Wars* the view of technology is further developed. There is a fascination and awe at technology, and of course technology itself is necessary to making the movies. However, technology becomes bad when it rules out spirituality. In the Empire, the machine seems to be the master. The Death Star is the ultimate symbol of technological progress out of control.

Throughout, this is contrasted with the power of the Force. One of the Imperial generals taunts Vader about his 'faith in ancient religion' contrasted with the power of the Death Star. Yet ultimately the Death Star is destroyed by trust in the Force.

The question is, Are humans enslaved or freed by technology? The Empire's reliance on technology is dehumanising. The biggest thing in the Empire is a weapon. Inside it is a cold and sterile environment. For all its vastness, the Death Star has no furniture and relatively few people. The stormtroopers seem dehumanised by their armour and loyalty to the system, showing unbelievable levels of ignorance and stupidity. Part of Darth Vader's inhumanity is shown by the fact that he is part human and part machine.

Joseph Campbell comments, 'Star Wars has a valid mythological perspective. It shows the state as a machine and asks, "Is the machine going to crush humanity or serve humanity?" Humanity comes not from the machine but from the heart.'[135]

Yet technology has its good side also. The Rebels use the technology against evil. The two droids central to the story, R2-D2 and C-3PO, are more 'human' than the stormtroopers, displaying human traits of loyalty, pride and joy. The journalist Ellen Goodman summed this up in one of the early reviews of Star Wars:

> The good guys are on the side of truth, beauty and
> cosmic force, but they aren't opposed to machines.
> Nor do they fight missiles with stones. The real battle
> is between one technological society that supports a
> Lone Rider and praises his instinct, and a technological
> society that over-rules individuals and suppresses
> instinct... Star Wars played out our own Good News
> and Bad News feelings about technology. We want a
> computer age with room for feelings. We want machines,
> but not the kind that run us. We want technology, but
> we want to be in charge of it.[136]

From Frankenstein to Dawkins

This is a theme that runs through not only *Star Wars*, but also through much of science fiction. Mary Shelley's *Frankenstein* (1818), argued by many to be the first science-fiction novel, reflected insights of the science of the day and asked the question, Where will this all lead? The ability to use electricity to move an animal's leg by stimulating the muscles could lead to Frankenstein sparking life into a manufactured creature.

The novel did not just explore such scientific ideas, but raised theological questions, such as, What is life? and What is creation? Shelley used a combination of rationalism and romanticism: human beings attempt to control the universe, but in the end become victims of their attempt.

The historian of science fiction, Brian Aldiss, writes, 'The concept of *Frankenstein* rests on the quasi-evolutionary idea that god is remote or absent from creation: man is therefore free to create his own sub-life.'[137] Shelley was an atheist and explored what it meant for humanity to replace or play God. Another historian of science fiction, Robert Reilly, has pointed out that until 1945 most science fiction viewed science as the key to all truth. Through science you could understand, manipulate, and then transcend, ordinary existence. In the works of authors such as Isaac Asimov and Arthur C. Clarke the vision of the future was one in which scientific progress leads to technological utopia.[138]

This view was strengthened by the increasing dominance of the so-called 'conflict hypothesis' of the relationship between science and religion. According to this view, science and religion were both describing the world in the same way and, where they differed, one had to be right and the other wrong. Thus, when a scientific theory of the origin of the universe, such as the Big Bang, came along and differed from the Genesis account, there was only one conclusion – the Genesis account must be wrong.

This conflict hypothesis was (and still is) very strong in Western culture. Created by T.H. Huxley at the turn of the twentieth century as part of a campaign to free science from the control of religion, it has many disciples today, including the eminent biologist and populariser of science, Richard Dawkins.

Science fiction thus began to contrast rationalist science with obscurantist religion. The novelist Kingsley Amis commented, 'When the sun seems about to turn into a nova, when the alien spacefleet closes in, when famine and pestilence follow in the wake of a nuclear war, prophets and fanatics impose themselves on the rabble while the scientists set their jaws and get on with the job.'[139]

As we have seen, this view was the basis of Gene Roddenberry's view of religion: god would be absent from the perfect future. Science had achieved harmony between races and cultures on the bridge of the starship *Enterprise*. Religion was evidence of psychological immaturity and science was the true saviour. Difficulties were conquered through Spock's rationalism and Scotty's ability with dilithium crystals without, of course, 'breaking the laws of physics'.

The trouble was that in the real world science failed to provide the utopia. As a result, a number of authors moved to religion and began to explore the transcendent. A new generation of science-fiction writers, such as Frank Herbert, began a personal search for absolute truth or transcendent reality. Religion was back in fashion. Writers created works in which symbolic or mythic patterns were instruments for exploring religion, evidenced by the work of C.S. Lewis.[140]

Star Wars took this trend onto the big screen. Pitting the Jedi belief in the Force against the technology of the Empire, Lucas once again raised the question of the transcendent. This was in line with the outlook of the science-fiction writer, Philip K. Dick, who followed Dostoevsky's view that 'the danger of man's self-destruction [lies] not in his failure to control the irrational but in his denial of its existence and his adulation of the rational'.[141]

In his study of the parallels of Christianity and science fiction, Stephen May suggests that they share a delight in otherness or transcendence.[142] That sense of the transcendent is fundamental to Star Wars, but it does not simply share it with Christianity: it derives a great deal from Christianity. The influence of George Lucas's early life and the general Western culture means that Star Wars strongly relies on the Christian concept of transcendence.

God and the Force

Lucas is quite explicit about his use of the Force. His emphasis on hope, on the responsibility of the individual, and the importance of morality, is based on belief in God. In the interview with Bill Moyers he says,

> Faith… is a very important part of what allows us to remain stable, remain balanced. I put the Force into the

movie in order to awaken a certain kind of spirituality in young people – more a belief in God than a belief in any particular religious system. I wanted to make it so that young people would begin to ask questions about the mystery. Not having enough interest in the mysteries of life to ask the question, 'Is there a God or is there not a God?' – that is for me is the worst thing that can happen. I think you should have an opinion about that. Or you should be saying, 'I'm looking. I'm very curious about this, and I am going to continue to look until I can find an answer, and if I can't find an answer, then I'll die trying.' I think it's important to have a belief system and to have faith.[143]

The emphasis on questions is very important in this. Lucas is not preaching the answers in *Star Wars*. That is the mistake of those who follow the 'religion of *Star Wars*'. The Force is not God and is not meant to have a rigorous scientific or theological justification. Those who believe that the Force is real are finding their answers in what are meant to be questions.

'I would hesitate to call the Force God,' says Lucas. 'It's designed primarily to make young people think about mystery. Not to say, "Here's the answer." It's to say, "Think about this for a second. Is there a God? What does God look like? What does God sound like? What does God feel like? How do we relate to God?"'[144] In that he has been enormously successful.

13

'Oh no, it's not like that at all. He's my brother'

The last line of *Return of the Jedi* is uttered by Leia concerning Luke. Their real relationship has been there for those who notice it, but it only becomes clear towards the end of the trilogy. The brother and sister born to Anakin Skywalker and Queen Amidala had no knowledge of each other even if their relationship always existed.

I have attempted in this book to suggest relationships between *Star Wars* and the Christian faith. I am not claiming in any way that the *Star Wars* concept is Christian, and that George Lucas is a cinematic Billy Graham. Instead I have argued that in a number of key areas *Star Wars* and Christianity share a common understanding:

1. Hope is to be found in transcendence rather than in human progress or technology.
2. Evil has to be combated both within and without the human individual.

3. In the concept of the hero, individual responsibility is recognised and encouraged, as a way to change society.

4. Redemption is achieved through self-sacrifice.

5. There is more to this universe than the things science can describe and manipulate.

I have also suggested that, in many respects, *Star Wars* derives images and motifs directly from Christianity and via the enduring legacy of Christianity in Western culture.

I find myself asking the question, Has this interpretation simply been imposed on *Star Wars*? After all, *Star Wars* has been interpreted in lots of ways by different religious views and at times these interpretations seem to go to extremes. For example, a recent author sees a reference to Jonah and the whale in *The Empire Strikes Back* when the *Millennium Falcon* is swallowed whole by a monster inside an asteroid. Furthermore, the swampland of the bog planet Dagobah and the barren wastelands of Tatooine symbolise aspects of the soul and the unconscious![145] Is this valid or just wishful thinking?

I readily acknowledge that I look on *Star Wars* from a Christian perspective. Part of my fascination with *Star Wars* has been the way that it resonates with my Christian belief. Yet I have tried to ground such resonances by going back to the ideas and words of George Lucas himself. On the basis of this, it is quite valid to take the religious aspects seriously.

At the heart of this approach is Lucas's own fundamental conviction that there is transcendence. He comments, 'All I was trying to say in a very simple and straightforward way is that there is a God and there is a good and bad side.'[146]

Furthermore, he says, 'I don't see *Star Wars* as profoundly religious. I see *Star Wars* as taking all the issues that religion represents and trying to distil them down into a more modern and easily accessible construct – that there is a great mystery out there.'[147]

It is this that gives *Star Wars* such a universal appeal. Taking a number of religious themes, not exclusively Christian, Lucas has told a story which raises questions in a way that people of different faiths and no faith can relate to.

Brains of a gnat and religious pornography?

The science-fiction writer Brian Aldiss once described *Star Wars* as 'an outsize elephant with the brains of a gnat'.[148] Others have been just as derogatory. Jacques Peretti writes, 'We live in a largely Godless culture. The Manichean mumbo-jumbo of *Star Wars* makes it perfect faith-lite for a soft-brained world. The mass hypnosis of *Star Wars* is very Diana-like. Just as we are now all capable of fake sentiment, so we are now all capable of fake deep.'[149] These words are reminiscent of the famous words of the science-fiction writer Stanislaw Lem who said of his own genre, 'Most science fiction is to authentic scientific, philosophical or theological knowledge as pornography is to love... Science fiction... removes itself from human concerns through deceptive ballyhoo.'[150]

Such criticism is unjust. The very success of *Star Wars* draws criticism. *Star Wars* is not just about special effects and merchandising, although they are part of the concept. It raises deep theological questions in a popular way.

The death of Diana, Princess of Wales, did not lead to mass hypnosis. As I saw packed churches in the UK and talked to many people with no connection to organised religion, the significance of her death was that it broke through the humanistic optimism and the glamour of the media world. The stark images of death reminded people of their own sadness in bereavement and raised deep questions. Unable to find a place within traditional churches to express these spiritual questions and emotions, people nevertheless wanted the opportunity to engage with them.

Star Wars fulfils a similar function. It is not the pornography of religion. It simply sets out to be a popular way of raising philosophical and theological questions.

There is an arrogance and perhaps jealousy around among various academics concerning the popular level of Star Wars. The Cambridge theologian Don Cupitt questions the value of science fiction. He suggests that interweaving scientific and religious ideas produces a kind of mythology or science fiction which is in fact both 'bad science and bad religion'.[151] One wonders just how much science fiction Cupitt has actually looked at. Some science fiction produces bad science and bad religion, but not all. Understood within its own genre, science fiction can stimulate the imagination in the areas of both science and religion. In fact, because of this, the philosopher Stephen Clark calls it, 'our century's greatest gift to literature'.[152] Indeed in the light of Star Wars he could have added 'to cinema' as well.

Star Wars removes itself from everyday concerns to reflect the big issues. A letter to The Guardian, responding to an article mocking Star Wars and Lucas, said, 'What Star Wars fans are so eager to embrace is the supernatural currency lost in modern bureaucracies – the magic of fantasies, transcendence and just plain mystery.'[153] That is its attraction. The popularity of *Star Wars* shows a generation searching for a new spirituality.

The search for spirituality

The critic Mark Lawson recently asked, Why is *Star Wars* so popular and so successful?[154] Why has it 'gone beyond entertainment'? He suggested six reasons. First, he suggested that the movies of Spielberg and Lucas were basically children's movies, which allowed adults to regress. Second, *Star Wars* was a movie about extraterrestrial intelligence, a subject which allows people to dream of leaving the Earth in the future. Third, he pointed out a political theme, which put together Kennedy's dream of humans in command of space with Ronald Reagan's nightmare, that is invasion by the Soviets. Fourth, *Star Wars* keys into the theme of dysfunctional families, which for increasing numbers of people speaks to their situation. Fifth, *Star Wars* brings nostalgia for the seventies, celebrated in recent years through movies like *Boogie Nights*, *Jackie Brown*, and the revival of the music of groups like Abba.

These five reasons have something to them. However, they do not explain the worldwide appeal of *Star Wars*. Lawson's sixth reason does. He suggests that *Star Wars* reflects a craving for religion.

The decline of traditional Christianity in the West has contributed to the search for alternatives. The collection of many ideas which go under the title 'New Age' gives a fertile ground for questions about spirituality. They have in common the rejection of the materialistic and mechanistic world-view so dominant since the time of Newton. The Newtonian world-view saw the universe as totally predictable, rather like the mechanism of a clock; described by science, it has no place for mystery, prayer or surprise.

The growth of the New Age in terms of the interest in astrology, channelling, crystals, meditation and nature worship shows an inner dissatisfaction at the technological world which seems to deny the spiritual. The expression of a universal religious sense, in reaction to its suppression in the modern Western world, finds outlets in paranormal experiences. The New Age movement protests that there is more to the universe than just an improbable evolution of a species totally alone in a mechanistic, impersonal universe.

Another area in which there is a search for spirituality is in that of belief in intelligent life elsewhere in the universe. This area, whether it be in science, science fiction or belief in alien visitation, has seen a massive growth of interest in the last decade. This is listed as Lawson's second reason for the appeal of *Star Wars*, but it is an expression of something deeper, linked to his sixth reason. From an extensive survey of the motivation behind scientific research into the existence of extraterrestrial intelligence, the belief in alien visitation and abduction, and contemporary science fiction, I have elsewhere suggested that people want to believe because of:[155]

- a sense of cosmic loneliness
- a search for cosmic purpose

- a search for human identity
- a sense of cosmic fear
- a need of cosmic salvation.

People seem unable to accept Jacques Monod's statement that, 'Man at last knows that he is alone in the unfeeling immensity of the universe.' We want to feel that we are part of something bigger, which gives us a wider perspective. *Star Trek* offers a future of humanity as part of a United Federation of Planets. *Star Wars* offers the sense of another galactic civilisation in the past.

We want to know whether there is a bigger story to our existence, whether in our history, our geography or our future. The cosmologist and populariser of science, Paul Davies, rightly sees this interest as coming from 'the need to find a wider context for our lives than this earthly existence provides. In an era when conventional religion is in sharp decline, the belief in super-advanced aliens out there somewhere in the universe can provide some measure of comfort and inspiration for people whose lives may otherwise appear to be boring and futile.'[156]

Star Wars picks up on this, giving a wider perspective not just in terms of other beings, but also the spiritual. Natalie Portman, who plays Queen Amidala in *The Phantom Menace*, comments that *Star Wars* has mythical and religious implications in that it addresses questions of 'meaning and hope'.[157] Dale Pollock writes that *Star Wars* is, 'a timeless fable that could demonstrate, not pontificate on, the differences between right and wrong, good and evil, responsibility and shiftlessness'.[158] He continues, 'Lucas is dealing with the big issues here, God and the Devil, good and evil, and the ways he illustrates them resonate in movie-goers' minds. Film is a perishable medium, but the images stay with us, becoming part of the way we define ourselves.'[159]

Now I am not suggesting that immediately after a showing of *The Phantom Menace* people will spontaneously form philosophy seminars or feel the urge to go to church on Sunday. Cinema does not work like that. John May helpfully points out that, 'Movies are felt by the audience long before they are "understood", if indeed they are ever fully understood.'[160] *Star Wars* addresses the emotions as well as the mind.

Movies also resonate with our own experiences. Sir Richard Attenborough recently commented on the way that cinema affected him: 'During the war I had two adopted German Jewish sisters – Irene and Helga. My family adopted them for various reasons and therefore the whole question of prejudice, tolerance and compassion is something that has always been with me… They were very much on my mind when I watched *Schindler's List*. I came out of that film and almost couldn't stand up.'

The popularity of *Star Wars* shows a deep hunger for spirituality within our Western society. It resonates with the desire to ask deep questions and find meaning and purpose in life.

Did you hear that?

From the very start of the *Star Wars* saga I have suggested that the spiritual is a key part, and indeed some of the understanding of the spiritual comes from the Christian tradition. George Lucas believes in the existence of God and tries to live his life in the light of that, saying, 'I am simply trying to struggle through life; trying to do God's bidding.'[161] Apart from being described as a 'Buddhist–Methodist,'[162] he does not claim a religious affiliation and, as we have seen, *Star Wars* is not a specifically Christian story.

Yet if some of the major influences on *Star Wars* are Christian, then what are the differences? If Christians need to hear and recognise the search for spirituality going on outside their churches, then can those who are into *Star Wars* hear anything of value from those who are Christian?

In fact, if *Star Wars* raises some of the questions, then Christianity offers some answers. This has been my experience, both as a teenager and now as someone who has done some science and some theology. Referring back to the questions that Lucas poses at the end of the previous chapter, we can see what the Christian faith can say to the story of *Star Wars*.

What is God like?

It is one thing to believe in the transcendent but the resulting question is perhaps even more important, 'What is God like?' Lucas expresses it himself: 'I think there is a God. No question. What that God is or what we know about that God, I'm not sure.'[163] How can we have sure knowledge about God? The only way would be if God himself revealed that knowledge to us.

Stephen May writes, 'The fourth-century theologian Athanasius made a vital distinction between "theology" and "mythology". According to this, theology is language "about" God based on the language "of" God – that is, given to us by God so that we may speak about him accurately. Mythology, by contrast, consists of stories we invent off the top of our own heads to try and make sense of a puzzling universe.'[164]

Star Wars is a modern mythology created by George Lucas. Christianity claims to be based on God revealing himself to us, supremely in the person of Jesus Christ. So, in answer to the question, What is God like? Christians reply that he is like Jesus.

How do we relate to God?

In his interview with Bill Moyers, Lucas comments on the advice that Obi-Wan Kenobi gives to Luke, who switches off his targeting computer during the attack on the Death Star in *Star Wars: A New Hope*: 'That is what that "Use the Force" is, a leap of faith. There are mysteries and powers larger than we are, and you have to trust your feelings in order to access them.'[165]

Christianity would partly agree and partly disagree. A leap of faith is seen as an act of trust in Jesus Christ. This may involve feelings – in terms of a particular experience of the love or peace of God. It also involves reason – the trust is on the basis of God revealing himself in history in the person of Jesus.

Trust also involves obedience. A Christian is a person who

follows Jesus and follows his teaching. In contrast with the Force, Jesus cannot be controlled. He is an active power for good and the appropriate response to his love is obedience. This relationship is not just for special people, that is those who have 'high concentrations of midi-chlorians' or are trained as Jedi Knights, but is for everyone who is prepared to trust.

Of course, at this point, the cost of being a Christian becomes obvious. It is fulfilling and exciting to be a Christian, but it is not a way to try to control the world. The follower of Jesus is pledged to work for peace and justice, reconciliation and the salvation of others. Following the one who gave himself as a sacrifice for others on the cross begs the question of whether we would do the same.

Is there a God?

What's the evidence for all of this belief? Isn't Christianity just a myth like *Star Wars*, created by people who wanted to try to understand and express the inexpressible? Surely one person can believe in *Star Wars* and another person believe in Christianity and there is no difference? If *Star Wars* is fantasy, then isn't Christianity just the same?

Christianity speaks of hope, the triumph of good, the responsibility of the individual and the transcendent. But it bases that not on a story but on the evidence of history. The core of the Christian belief – of hope, the defeat of evil and a relationship with God which gives help and strength now – is the resurrection of Jesus. The evidence is not just the billion or so Christians in the world today who speak of some kind of experience of the risen Jesus, or those throughout the centuries who speak of the same kind of experience. The evidence is the historical events surrounding the death and claimed resurrection of Jesus.

These include the fact of the empty tomb, the appearances of the risen Jesus to over 500 people within forty days, the growth of the early church, and the transformation of the disciples. The evidence of history does not give proof. You have to weigh the evidence and make a judgment. And I have to say, in my view, the historical evidence for the resurrection of Jesus is overwhelming.

Joseph Campbell wrote,

We do not particularly care whether Rip van Winkle, Kamar al-Zaman, or Jesus Christ ever actually lived. Their stories are what concern us: and these stories are so widely distributed over the world… that the question of whether this or that local carrier of the universal theme may or may not have been a historical, living man can be of only secondary moment. The stressing of this historical element will lead to confusion; it will simply obfuscate the picture message.[166]

Campbell misunderstands the Christian message. It is because the story of Jesus is firmly located in historical fact that we can be sure about hope and the victory of good over evil.

As we have seen in Chapter 5, one of the fascinating aspects of *Star Wars* merchandise are the books and CD-ROMs which go into detail about a fantasy story: How do the starships work? Where are the planets in the galaxy? I bet there is even some book somewhere which tells you what Jedi Knights eat for breakfast! I think part of what is going on here is that people are looking for evidence, subconsciously wanting this to be real rather than fantasy. We have also seen that the special effects encourage people to believe that it is real. People want evidence to undergird the hope and meaning.

Christianity offers that. It also offers involvement. The person at Twentieth Century Fox who backed George Lucas and made *Star Wars* possible was Alan Ladd, Jr. He said of Lucas, 'He showed people it was alright to become totally involved in a movie again; to yell and scream and applaud and really roll with it.'[167] The movie does invite involvement. The toys and games amplify this, encouraging you to become part of the story.

Christianity also makes such an invitation, but not for a couple of hours in a darkened cinema, or in front of a PC screen, but day by day for the whole of life. To trust and obey Jesus involves me in a bigger story about God working out his purposes in some small way through me. As I have tried to live in that kind of way I have begun to discover just how real God is.

I have written this book to try to analyse the success of *Star Wars* and its relationship to Christianity. My hope is that those who are Christians may see *Star Wars* in a new light and see the spiritual hunger that lies behind its success. For those who are not Christians, and who are fascinated by *Star Wars*, I hope that they will see that Christianity offers answers to some of the questions that Lucas poses. Whether those answers have credibility and evidence needs to be checked out in ways beyond the scope of this book.

The wonder of *Star Wars*

I return to a question which was posed to me during a radio interview: 'Surely *Star Wars* is just entertainment and nothing to do with theology?' It is an interesting question and actually exposes a fundamental misunderstanding. It makes entertainment and theology two mutually exclusive things and assumes that theology is the more worthwhile thing.

If *Star Wars* has been derided for being crude and childish, then Christianity was also. It was at first regarded with disdain by the intellectuals.[168] Some regarded it as fit only for slaves and women, and Augustine struggled with taunts from educated pagans about the unsophisticated gospels. It was too popular for some. The New Testament was written in common Greek, the mystery plays brought Christianity to the masses at the most crude and ribald level, and hymn writers such as Charles Wesley used the tunes to popular contemporary songs in the eighteenth century to express praise to God.

In many ways, theology and entertainment have often been woven together. J.R.R. Tolkien's *The Lord of the Rings* (1954–55) was based on Christian foundations, and C.S. Lewis expressed his orthodox beliefs though science fiction and fantasy. Indeed, Jesus himself used stories to teach about the kingdom of God. Parables such as that of the lost sheep were entertainment. The audience would have laughed at how thick the shepherd was to leave ninety-nine sheep and go after the one that was lost! In their laughter, however, they would begin to see the intensity of the love of God for the individual within the image.

Parables were images of the kingdom of God, open to interpretation, but accessible to everyone who wanted to find out more. Ultimately parables were invitations to think through the issues for yourself. More direct proclamation, which Jesus also did, is usually either resisted or simply accepted at an intellectual level without any commitment. Parables entertain but they also invite the listener to use their imagination to get involved in the story, but with a degree of serious commitment. *Star Wars* is not far from being a parable – not about the kingdom of God, but about the existence of God.

Stephen May argues that the emotional heart of science fiction is wonder. He writes, 'Wonder stands at the beginning of the science-fiction experience.'[169] *Star Wars* engenders wonder, from the special effects to the power of the Force. As it does that, it acts as a mirror to who we are, but also points beyond us to possibilities of where we could be.

It may not go as far as theological enquiry but, using this sense of wonder in a story containing religious themes, it encourages us to use our imagination and think about the questions.

Francis Coppola once advised George Lucas, when the success of the *Star Wars* series became known, that rather than extend the sequence he should found a religion with the scripts as scriptures. 'Religion is where the real power is,' he is reported to have said to Lucas. Lucas wisely declined the advice. He knew that in fact cinema has a power to express religion in a way that frees people to use their imagination. The wonder of *Star Wars* is much more powerful than the cold sterility of many formal acts of worship.

Douglas Coupland, who coined the phrase 'Generation X', wrote, 'My secret is that I need God – that I am sick and can no longer make it alone. I need God to help me give, because I no longer seem to be capable of giving; to help me be kind, as I no longer seem capable of kindness; to help me love, as I seem beyond being able to love.'[170]

In the midst of the angst of Vietnam, Watergate, the Cold War and the hunger for spiritual experience, *Star Wars* became the most successful series of movies ever. Today in a postmodern generation that needs to experience truth rather than have it stated, the wonder of *Star Wars* finds fertile ground to raise the question of God.

It may not be Shakespeare but, in the words of the actor Brian Blessed, its legacy to the 'civilised development of the human race' is an exciting and fun story of hope based on a belief in a transcendent reality. If that is the underlying meaning of 'May the Force be with you,' then it may not be too ridiculous after all.

Suggestions for further reading

L. Bouzereau and J. Duncan, *Star Wars Episode I: Making of The Phantom Menace*, Special Collector's Limited Edition (London: Ebury, 1999).

M.S. Henderson, *Star Wars: The Magic of Myth* (New York: Bantam, 1997).

C. Marsh and G. Ortiz, *Explorations in Theology and Film* (Oxford: Blackwell, 1998).

S. May, *Stardust and Ashes: Science Fiction in Christian Perspective* (London: SPCK, 1998).

S.J. Sansweet, *Star Wars: From Concept to Screen to Legend* (San Francisco: Chronicle, 1992).

B. Slavicsek, *A Guide to the Star Wars Universe* (London: Boxtree, 1995).

D. Wilkinson, *Alone in the Universe? The X-Files, Aliens and God* (Crowborough: Monarch, 1996).

Endnotes

1: Every journey has a first step

1. A. Guinness, *A Positively Final Appearance* (London: Hamish Hamilton, 1999), p. 11.
2. T. Rayment, *The Sunday Times*, 16 May 1999.
3. Rayment, ibid.
4. *Total Film*, April 1997.
5. 'Star Wars, 1977–1997: The Legend', *Empire*, April 1997.
6. *Empire*, ibid.
7. B. Logan, *The Guardian*, 6 April 1999.
8. Guinness, op. cit. (1), p. 11.
9. S. Vine, *The Times*, 22 May 1999.
10. G. Morris, *The Guardian*, 22 May 1999.
11. D. Pollock, *Skywalking: The Life and Films of George Lucas* (Hollywood: Samuel French, 1990), p. xii.
12. M.S. Henderson, *Star Wars: The Magic of Myth* (New York: Bantam, 1997), p. 3.
13. R. Rayner, *The Sunday Telegraph*, 28 March 1999.
14. Rayment, op. cit. (2).
15. Pollock, op. cit. (11), p. 139.

2: The beginning

16. Pollock, op. cit. (11), p. 148.
17. Pollock, op. cit. (11), p. 175.
18. J.P. Peecher (ed.), *The Making of Star Wars, Return of the Jedi* (New York: Ballantine, 1983), p. 237.
19. C. Salewicz, *George Lucas Close Up* (London: Orion, 1998), p. 125.
20. Peecher, op. cit. (18), p. 240.
21. Salewicz, op. cit. (19), p. 129.
22. *Variety*, 18 May 1983.
23. B. Slavicsek, *A Guide to the Star Wars Universe* (London: Boxtree, 1995), p. xviii.

3: 'Don't underestimate the Force'

24. Rayment, op. cit. (2).
25. Quoted in D. Alexander, *Star Trek Creator – The Authorised Biography of Gene Roddenberry* (London: Boxtree, 1994), p. 521.
26. See J. Mitchell, *The Month*, May 1998, p. 175.
27. A. Lane, *The Babylon File: The Definitive Unauthorised Guide to J. Michael Stracsynski's TV Series, Babylon 5* (London: Virgin, 1997).
28. C. Marsh and G. Ortiz, *Explorations in Theology and Film* (Oxford: Blackwell, 1998).

4: *The Phantom Menace* and fandom mania

29. *USA Today*, 20 May 1999.
30. *Heat*, 29 May 1999.
31. *The Observer*, 16 May 1999.
32. G. Lucas, *Star Wars Episode I: The Phantom Menace, The Illustrated Screenplay* (London: Ebury, 1999), p. 61.
33. Lucas, ibid., p. 97.
34. Lucas, ibid., p. 83.
35. Lucas, ibid., p. 105.
36. Lucas, ibid., p. 108.

5: May the market force be with you

37. S.J. Sansweet, *Star Wars: From Concept to Screen to Legend* (San Francisco: Chronicle, 1992), p. 67.
38. B. Moyers and G. Lucas, 'Of Myth and Men', *Time*, 26 April 1999.
39. Peecher, op. cit. (18), p. 72.
40. L. Bouzereau and J. Duncan, *Star Wars Episode I: Making of The Phantom Menace*, Special Collector's Limited Edition (London: Ebury, 1999), p. 87.
41. Pollock, op. cit. (11), p. 193.

6: 'Every generation has a legend...'

42. Peecher, op. cit. (18), p. 228.
43. Pollock, op. cit. (11), p. 19.

44. Pollock, op. cit. (11), p. 20.

45. Pollock, op. cit. (11), p. xxii.

46. Pollock, op. cit. (11), p. xix.

47. Salewicz, op. cit. (19), p. 40.

48. Pollock, op. cit. (11), p. 104.

7: 'You've got something jammed in here real good'

49. Peecher, op. cit. (18), p. 237.

50. *Empire*, op. cit. (5).

51. J. Campbell, *The Hero with a Thousand Faces* (London: Fontana, 1993), p. 3.

52. J. Campbell and B. Moyers, *The Power of Myth* (New York: Doubleday, 1988).

53. B. Bettelheim, *The Uses of Enchantment* (London: Penguin, 1976).

54. C. Champlin, *George Lucas: The Creative Impulse* (London: Virgin, 1997), p. 124.

55. Campbell and Moyers, op. cit. (52), p. 126.

56. *Empire*, op. cit. (5).

57. Moyers and Lucas, op. cit. (38).

58. Henderson, op. cit. (12), p. 133.

59. Salewicz, op. cit. (19), p. 24.

60. B. Aldiss, *Space Opera* (London: Futura, 1974), p. 10.

61. R. Slotkin, *Gunfighter Nation: The Myth of the Frontier in Twentieth-Century America* (New York: Harper Perennial, 1993), p. 349.

62. *Empire*, op. cit. (5).

63. Henderson, op. cit. (12), p. 136.

64. *Empire*, op. cit. (5).
65. Moyers and Lucas, op. cit. (38).
66. Campbell and Moyers, op. cit. (52), p. 144.
67. E. Durkheim, *The Elementary Forms of the Religious Life*, tr. J.W. Swain (London: George Allen and Unwin, 1915), p. 37.
68. Henderson, op. cit. (12), p. 198.
69. Pollock, op. cit. (11), p. 140.
70. Pollock, op. cit. (11), p. 140.
71. Henderson, op. cit. (12), p. 10.
72. O. Schell, *The Observer Review*, 25 April 1999.
73. Moyers and Lucas, op. cit. (38).
74. *Empire*, op. cit. (5).
75. S. Zito, 'Far Out', *American Film*, March 1977.

8: A new hope

76. Peecher, op. cit. (18), p. 236.
77. Salewicz, op. cit. (19), p. 101.
78. See, for example, R. Bauckham and T. Hart, *Hope Against Hope: Christian Eschatology in Contemporary Context* (London: DLT, 1999).
79. S. May, *Stardust and Ashes: Science Fiction in Christian Perspective* (London: SPCK, 1998).
80. J. Moltmann, *Theology of Hope* (London: SCM, 1967), pp. 7, 23f.
81. W. Irwin, *The Game of the Impossible: A Rhetoric of Fantasy* (Illinois: University of Illinois Press, 1976), p. x.
82. Pollock, op. cit. (11), p. 158.
83. F. Kermode, *The Sense of an Ending* (London: OUP, 1967).

84. G. Steiner, *Real Presences: Is There Anything in What We Say?* (London: Faber, 1989), p. 227.
85. Bauckham and Hart, op. cit. (78), p. 51.
86. Moltmann, op. cit. (80), p. 21.
87. Bauckham and Hart, op. cit. (78), p. 36.
88. B. Bettelheim, 'The Art of Moving Pictures', *Harper's Magazine*, October 1981, p. 82.
89. Salewicz, op. cit. (19), p. 44.

9: 'Aren't you a little short for a stormtrooper?'

90. G. Lucas, *Star Wars: From the Adventures of Luke Skywalker* (London: Sphere, 1977), p. 6.
91. Campbell, op. cit. (51), p. 249.
92. Campbell and Moyers, op. cit. (52), p. 144.
93. C.S. Lewis, 'On Science Fiction' (1955), *Of This and Other Worlds: Essays and Stories* (London: Collins, 1982), p. 87.
94. Moyers and Lucas, op. cit. (38).
95. Richard Carliss, 'Ready, Set, Glow', *Time*, 31 May 1999, p. 57.
96. Schell, op. cit. (72).
97. Schell, op. cit. (72).
98. *Empire*, op. cit. (5).
99. *Empire*, op. cit. (5).

10: 'The boy is dangerous...'

100. *Empire*, op. cit. (5).
101. Henderson, op. cit. (12), p. 116.

102. Henderson, op. cit. (12), p. 120.

103. Moyers and Lucas, op. cit. (38).

104. Moyers and Lucas, op. cit. (38).

105. Moyers and Lucas, op. cit. (38).

106. Campbell and Moyers, op. cit. (52), p. 145.

107. Henderson, op. cit. (12), p. 120.

108. D. Wilkinson, *God, the Big Bang and Stephen Hawking* (Crowborough: Monarch, 1996).

109. *Omnibus*, BBC TV, 7 July 1999.

110. *Omnibus*, ibid.

11: 'I will grow more powerful than you can possibly imagine...'

111. Campbell and Moyers, op. cit. (52), p. 144.

112. Moyers and Lucas, op. cit. (38).

113. Moyers and Lucas, op. cit. (38).

114. *Empire*, op. cit. (5).

115. Henderson, op. cit. (12), p. 120.

116. M. Wright, 'Moses at the Movies: Ninety Years of the Bible and Film', *Modern Believing*, vol. 37/1, pp. 46–54, 1996.

117. G. Ortiz, 'Jesus at the Movies: Cinematic Representation of the Christ-figure', *The Month*, December 1994.

118. Ortiz, ibid.

119. Isaiah 53:5 (NIV).

120. John 15:13 (NRSV).

121. F. Hoyle, *Monthly Notices of the Royal Astronomical Society*, vol. 109, p. 365, 1949.

12: Feel the Force

122. Guinness, op. cit. (1), p. 12.

123. *Omnibus*, op. cit. (109).

124. D. Pringle, *The Ultimate Guide to Science Fiction* (London: Grafton, 1990).

125. S. Athorne, 'The Lexicon of Lucas', *The Sunday Times*, 16 May 1999.

126. S.J. Sansweet, *Star Wars Encyclopedia* (Virgin, 1998).

127. T. Brooks, *Star Wars Episode I: The Phantom Menace* (London: Century, 1999), p. 27.

128. Brooks, ibid., p. 241.

129. Salewicz, op. cit. (19), p. 48.

130. May, op. cit. (79), p. 37.

131. C.J. Cherryh, 'Goodbye Star Wars, Hello Alley-oop', in S. Jarvis (ed.), *Inside Outer Space: Science-fiction Professionals Look at Their Craft* (New York: Ungar, 1985), p. 17.

132. Peecher, op. cit. (18), p. 198.

133. Zito, op. cit. (75).

134. Schell, op. cit. (72).

135. Campbell and Moyers, op. cit. (52), p. 8.

136. E. Goodman, *Washington Post*, 30 July 1977, A15.

137. B. Aldiss, *Billion Year Spree: The History of Science Fiction* (London: Corgi, 1973), p. 29.

138. R. Reilly, *The Transcendent Adventure, Studies of Religion in Science Fiction/ Fantasy* (Westport: Greenwood, 1985).

139. K. Amis, *New Maps of Hell: A Survey of Science Fiction* (London: Gollancz, 1961), p. 83.

140. C.S. Lewis, *Perelandra* (London: John Lane, 1943).

141. May, op. cit. (79), p. 56.

142. May, op. cit. (79), p. 116.

143. Moyers and Lucas, op. cit. (38).

144. Moyers and Lucas, op. cit. (38).

13: 'Oh no, it's not like that at all. He's my brother'

145. Salewicz, op. cit. (19), p. 103.

146. Salewicz, op. cit. (19), p. 47.

147. Moyers and Lucas, op. cit. (38).

148. B. Aldiss with D. Wingrove, *Trillion Year Spree* (London: Gollancz, 1961), p. 271.

149. J. Peretti, *The Guardian*, 10 July 1999.

150. E. James, *Science Fiction and the Twentieth Century* (Oxford: OUP, 1994), p. 144.

151. D. Cupitt, *Only Human* (London: SCM, 1985), p. 48.

152. S.R.L. Clark, *How to Live Forever: Science Fiction and Philosophy* (London: Routledge, 1995), p. 5.

153. *The Guardian*, 29 May 1999, p. 25. Letter from Simon Werrett, Cambridge, in response to article by Gabrielle Morris, 'Hall of Infamy, No. 23', 22 May 1999.

154. M. Lawson, *The Guardian Weekend*, 24 April 1999.

155. D. Wilkinson, *Alone in the Universe? The X-Files, Aliens and God* (Crowborough: Monarch, 1996).

156. P. Davies, *Are We Alone?* (London: Penguin, 1995), p. 89.

157. *Omnibus*, op. cit. (109).

158. Pollock, op. cit. (11), p. 139.

159. Pollock, op. cit. (11), p. 272.

160. J.R. May (ed.), *Image and Likeness: Religious Visions in American Film Classics* (Mahwah/New York: Paulist, 1992), p. 3.

161. Pollock, op. cit. (11), p. 141.

162. Rayner, op. cit. (13).

163. Moyers and Lucas, op. cit. (38).

164. May, op. cit. (79), p. 120.

165. Moyers and Lucas, op. cit. (38).

166. Campbell, op. cit. (51), pp. 230–31.

167. Pollock, op. cit. (11), p. 186.

168. E. Auerbach, *Mimesis: The Representation of Reality in Western Literature*, tr. W.R. Trask (Princeton: Princeton University, 1953).

169. May, op. cit. (79), p. 13.

170. D. Coupland, *Life After God* (New York: Pocket Books, 1994), p. 359.